Writing with God

The Transforming Intimacy
of the Soul Journal

Patrick Mayfield

Praise for *Writing with God*

In Writing with God, Patrick invites us to enjoy the privilege of a dynamic, intimate and very personal conversation with God through journalling. Patrick's testimony and ability to share practical tips will inspire you! You will learn how to create a space free of noise and distraction that will enable you to converse with God- a beautiful space to be consciously aware of Him and be renewed as you interact with the most loving, joyful and wise God.

Rachel & Jamie Lee
Leaders of Church of Christ the King, Plumstead, UK
& authors of *God Doesn't Do Magic*

Ever wished you could hold up a mirror to your soul and be honest with yourself? Ever struggled with the distractions and noise of contemporary lifestyle? Ever wondered how you can grow more self-aware and God aware? Patrick's book Writing with God will help you do this and more. Harnessing the insights of neuroscience, the Bible and lessons from his own experience of journalling, he will help you develop your emotional intelligence, think about your thinking, develop your "focus muscles", hear God more clearly and reflect on what he is saying to you. Patrick has given us a concise and practical guide to spiritual journalling that will take you deeper in your relationship with the Father and help release you into greater creativity and freedom as a child of God. I commend his book to you as another great tool in helping you live a powerful Kingdom lifestyle.

David Webster
Author of *Your Royal Identity*, and Director at Eastgate

In Writing with God, Patrick not only sets out clearly how many of us, busy and distracted people, need the discipline of soul journalling; he also offers practical suggestions about beginning and sustaining it. His book has blessed and encouraged me to return to this helpful spiritual discipline after almost two years' absence.

Richard Smith
Change Consultant &
Lead Author of *The Effective Change Manager's Handbook*

The Greek philosopher Socrates once stated that, "The unexamined life is not worth living." If ever there was an ancient observation that has become a maxim for our day, then this probably is it. The speed, noise and distraction of the present day has robbed the modern believer of one of the most important and joyful disciplines… journeying with God in the quiet place. Writing with God is a great antidote to the enemies of this journey. For the Jews of Jesus' day, the wilderness was the 'place of speaking' - the place of intimacy - the place of preparation. In this book, Patrick skilfully reconnects us with the ancient path of journeying with God in the quiet place, all the while, holding to the reality of the modern world we find ourselves walking in. This book will be pure gold to any who want to walk with God and grow deeper in Him but need a helping hand to get going!

Mark Hendley
Biblical Historian & Teacher, KingdomCollision.com

What a wonderful book — inspirational but also challenging and profoundly practical. I love the way Patrick invites me from a world of distraction and internal chatter to a place of deep thinking, where I can journal my interior world and God's interactions with me. Most importantly reading this book has given me the impetus to pick up my pen and restart my practice of daily journalling — something I have always valued but has slipped away in recent times.

Katy Dusting
Life Coach and Spiritual Director

Dedication

To my late mother.

Mum, I owe you more than you know.

&

To Michael & Julia.

Michael, we miss you.
Looking forward to seeing you again in the life to come.

Julia, In the words of Jenn Johnson,
"Hold on. You're Gonna Be OK" x

Foreword

I am so glad that Patrick has written a book about journalling. I have now been keeping a journal since March 2016. By that point I had been a Christian for almost 30 years. Like many of us (I suspect) I had often heard people speak about the benefits of journalling – whether that be writing out your prayers, or simply keeping a diary. However, for whatever reason, I had not got around to actually doing it in a disciplined way.

Similarly with my Bible reading. I love the word, and when I was first saved I read and re-read the Bible. But I had come to a point where I needed something to help me to engage with God's word afresh and feel it impact my daily life.

The tool that I needed was given to me by my good friend Mark Appleyard who introduced me to SOAP journalling (which Patrick covers in Chapter 5). The simple structure of Scripture, Observation, Application, Prayer, has honestly changed my life.

I am so impressed by Patrick. He is the author of several books, and yet he is humble and so willing (eager even) to learn from others. When I taught some sessions at the Eastgate School of Spiritual Life a couple of years ago, Patrick (who is an experienced teacher and presenter) told me that he had decided to copy my format in classes he then taught, as it had worked so well. When I introduced the concept of SOAP journalling, Patrick – who (as you will learn) had been journalling for many years - came and told me weeks later that it had transformed his journalling.

This book has influenced me. For three years I have been journalling on the computer, which has many advantages. But the encouragement to consider the advantages of using a pen and a physical journal convinced me to try it again and I have now been journalling over a month in this way. (I will probably chop and change which is fine, good even.)

By reading this book you will benefit from the many, many insights which Patrick has gained as he has walked out his own journalling journey and as he has had the humility and the wisdom to eagerly learn from others, and the generosity to share that knowledge with others.

I am proud, in the best sense of the word, to have Patrick as my friend and I thoroughly commend this book to you. If you apply these insights and tools to your life you will start (or continue) a journey where the rewards are great. What could be greater than hearing God's voice and knowing His presence? Happy Journalling!

Rob Schulz

Director of Gladwyn Enterprises and Kingdom Leader

Preface

Sometimes I can be so close to something, so familiar with it, that I don't even notice it, let alone value it. For a long time, I didn't see the power in my life of this thing that I came to call my soul journal.

It was a practice born out of a mild desperation.

Then, desperation turned into delight. Through the pages of a journal, I discovered a powerful medium to talk with God.

This book was not what I had started to write. I began to write a book about reflective writing. It morphed into this one you are reading right now.

As I talked with others about this, I found many who had stumbled upon this phenomenon as well. I found such potency in the practice of soul journalling and such a confirmation from others around me that I felt Abba wanted me to write this book.

It was time for me to make some sense of what was happening.

....

Before I begin, though, if you don't have a living faith in Christ, I urge you to seek him. As I read the gospels, it is clear to me that the closest associates of Jesus, his disciples, at first really didn't know who he was or where he was taking them. If this is where you are on your spiritual journey, then maybe this book will help you.

And then you might be a Christ-follower, but you do not get along at all with writing or journalling; you might feel closer to God when you are walking, exercising or working in a hot, noisy kitchen, as was the case with Brother Lawrence. If you are that kind of disciple, then God bless you. You may want to put this book down and carry on. We are each gloriously unique, and our uniqueness is to be valued and celebrated. This book is not an implied mandate that every believer must soul journal.

However, as my friend and mentor, Vicky Schulz, pointed out to me,

> I think God is always looking for new ways to speak to all of us, and there is value in everyone giving it a try.

So, you might want to do just that: try it!

Also, if you believe that God will *only* speak to you through the Bible, then this book is unlikely to persuade you otherwise; indeed, it is not meant to argue theology in the absence of relationship, although it does contain theology. (Hint: you have already read some of it.)

I invite you into a wonderfully dynamic experience of how we can relate to God on the page, in a way that is complementary to all the traditional practices of Christians.

So I write for people who are already on a relational journey with our amazing God, and might be considering journalling in some way. Maybe you have journaled before in the past, and have allowed this practice to lapse, and perhaps never considered it as an intimate arena of discipleship, of conversation with God. Allow me to light that fire for you.

Patrick Mayfield
September 2019
Kent, UK

Contents

CHAPTER 1

Hello?

"Well, I was talking with him only this morning..."

I was coming towards the end of my gap year between school and college, and something unexpected happened.

I had saved enough money working as a school caretaker to visit my cousin in Toronto. I was looking forward to it. I was eager to join in with whatever many in my age group were doing in those days, such as experimenting with drugs, music and sex.

When I arrived in Canada, I found myself in the middle of something very strange. It was strange but yet familiar. I was later to realise that it was a revival among hippies like me, that was sweeping across North America. It was later called the Jesus People movement. In fact, my cousin had left drug-dealing to become one of them.

My reaction? I explained that I was a Christian too! And so I went along with it.

I had been raised a Roman Catholic by my loving, godly mother. I always valued my faith, even being serious enough at one time as a teenager to become an MC or 'Master of Ceremonies' (aka. head altar boy) for a local convent. But for me it was mostly aesthetics, form, morality and a belief system. There was no intimacy with God as I now know it. I would defend my faith, but not with any real sense of knowing God personally. In the circles I had moved in, that kind of intimacy with the Almighty just wasn't on offer.

My cousin, his friend and I drove through southern Ontario in an old car, an Austin A40, trying to find the lakeside cabin of another friend's parents. We stopped at a beach on Lake Huron to ask for directions and found ourselves talking to a group of high school students who were part of a summer camp. They told us that in the course of the week so far, nearly all of them had had a powerful encounter with the living God. Out of a camp of 109 teenagers, over a hundred of them had already given their lives to Christ. I was experiencing revival.

So, they invited us back to the camp that evening to give our testimonies. I didn't even know what a 'testimony' was and, wisely perhaps, the leaders did not ask me to stand up and tell my story. But they did ask us each to lead a Bible study. I thought I would read up on this and bought a little booklet called *The Four Spiritual Laws*. That night, I began that booklet as a religious teenager, and finished it knowing this Jesus for myself.

It seems that I had led myself to Christ.

The way I describe that experience now was that it was as though I was a child playing with a telephone, and then someone on the other end answers and speaks to me! I was no longer pretending to communicate with God. Now, I was talking with him. Now, this all seems so relevant to the theme of this book: hearing God through journalling.

Ae UK a year after this happened to me, Billy Graham was in the UK. When asked by a reporter why he believed in God, he replied, "Well, I was talking with him only this morning." Believing in the existence of God is just not an issue when I am intimate with him each day.

The Religion Virus

> Now while [Zechariah] was serving as a priest before God
> when his division was on duty, according to the custom of the
> priesthood, he was chosen by lot to enter the temple of the Lord
> and burn incense. And the whole multitude of the people were
> praying outside at the hour of incense. And there appeared to
> him an angel of the Lord standing at the right hand of the altar
> of incense. And Zechariah was troubled when he saw him, and
> fear fell upon him… And the people were waiting for Zechariah,
> and they were wondering at his delay in the temple.
>
> Luke 1:8-12,21

I feel a little sorry for Zechariah. This moment was the zenith of his career as a professional priest, and God shows up in the form of an angel and disrupts it. God spoiled Zechariah's religious service.

My mother had done the best she knew how to lead me to a life of faith and devotion to God. However, I began to discover that the faith community that I had grown up in was essentially a humanly-organised one. If God didn't show up, we could carry on without thinking anything was amiss. I now call that **religion** as opposed to Christian discipleship.

Since then, I've talked with many Catholics who have encountered God personally, where he does show up supernaturally, and where they express a living faith, a dynamic relationship with their Creator. Until my encounter in the youth camp, I had only experienced religion, not relationship. So, as I moved into other church streams looking for that life and vitality, I realised that the roots of religion were not exclusive to Catholicism. I've found it since among Baptists, Buddhists and Brethren; among Methodists and Moslems; and among Anglicans, Pentecostals, and Jehovah Witnesses. I came to realise that religious thinking and practice was everywhere. When people thought of God and expressing belief in him, they immediately thought of some form of religion or rules of behaviour, rather than their living relationship and encounters with him.

Very soon though, I realised that the religion virus was still in me, and was blocking deeper growth in my intimacy with Jesus.

Leaven

> Jesus said to them, "Watch out and beware of the
> leaven of the Pharisees and Sadducees."
>
> Matthew 16:6

This leaven of the Pharisees was something that exercised Jesus enough to warn his disciples about it. It was the way he described the religion virus. On a good day, a Pharisee was someone who lived as a good person, as an outstanding member of the community. Most of the time, though, the culture of the Pharisees and Sadducees was hypocrisy, an external show that was profoundly discordant with their inner world. This leaven was all about performance and appearance. It was a leaven that would work its way through everything.

I had discovered and experienced grace. And through grace, relationship with the Author of the Universe; but I was in danger of being suckered again into performance religion.

So when I prayed, I lapsed into ways of praying that had been modelled for me by those I had seen praying and had looked up to as my mentors. I saw people saying their prayers, rather than talking with the living God. As a Catholic, I had been taught to say my rosary, a repetition of the Lord's prayer and the *Hail Mary*, multiple times, as a form of penance, petition and intercession. As I continued out of duty and performance, I slipped back into *saying* my prayers rather than *praying*. It felt lifeless. The more I prayed, the more boring it was. Every so often, I would take myself in hand, telling myself that praying was not for my entertainment; it was "the sacrifice of prayer."

Somehow I had to win this battle for prayer. It was the key to growing in my faith in God and to succeeding in life. But this didn't seem to be the way.

Prayer

Then, I read a book by Bill Hybels called, *Too Busy Not to Pray*.[1] I began to write out my prayers in a journal every day. Hybels recommended getting a spiral-bound notebook, writing one's reflections of the previous day on one page and writing out a prayer on the next.

At first, I found it a rather awkward, self-conscious affair. I remember I was quite bothered about who my audience was supposed to be. How much openness could I allow myself on the written page? What if someone read my journal? After all, I have some pretty unattractive thoughts and habits!

Nevertheless, the advice of Hybels was hugely helpful. I used to begin each daily entry with the reflective word, *Yesterday*. As I persevered, all of these concerns gradually fell away as I focused on other things, on just expressing myself on the page.

In fact, the whole process became deeply satisfying. So much so, that it became part of me. It was the basis from which I began to experiment with a God-focused journalling, what I now call soul journalling. I looked forward to my daily soul journalling with some anticipation and pleasure.

With the joy of journalling, came something else that was profoundly positive, something I didn't altogether appreciate at the time. I began to establish what Charles Duhigg calls a *Keystone Habit*, a habit that started to spin off and express itself in multiple other positive behaviours.[2] My prayer journalling spilled out into several other areas of my life.

This effect has had such a positive impact upon me that now, when I am coaching, I often ask my clients if they journal, or whether they have discovered and established a similar habit.

> Thoughts disentangle themselves when
> they pass through your fingertips.
> **Dawson Trotman**

Trotman's observation in this quote is profound. It could express much of what the rest of this book is about, but not everything. It does not explain the essence of soul journalling.

Here's what Nicole Adams wrote to me about the Trotman quote:

> I get revelation as I write. The thoughts disentangle but additionally revelation may be downloaded.

As I reflected on the page, I began to make sense of the noise in my head. Writing slowed me down. I began to think more deliberately and clearly. This practice became for me a powerful route to greater self-awareness, to what many now call mindfulness.

The Soul Journal

> Why are you cast down, O my soul,
> and why are you in turmoil within me?
> Hope in God; for I shall again praise him,
> my salvation and my God.
> **Psalm 42:5-6a**

In Psalm 42, the Sons of Korah wrote down how a man of God took his soul in hand. Reading this now, I realise that this psalm was a narrative of a person speaking to their own soul, strengthening themselves in the Lord, as David did another time at Ziklag (1 Samuel 30:6b).

Over time, my journal became a place where I could stand back and observe what was happening in my own soul; when I was ready to open up in my journal, I could put down on paper my recurring thoughts, hopes and fears. I could rehearse what I believed about God, the world and what was happening to me and through me.

This helped me enormously to sort out the muddle in my head. Even when I wasn't going through some big crisis or challenge, the journal helped me process my deeper thinking. I had already begun to explore my main priorities; so, writing down my daily thoughts helped me to see how aligned I was to these important things in my life. I studied more by reading what others said about journalling and writing.

I came across some work by teachers who were using writing in this way as a kind of cathartic exercise for creatives. As people allowed themselves to express their thoughts and emotions in writing, it began to unravel and clarify their inner world.

Later, someone in an online mastermind group I was part of referred me to the work of James Pennebaker and Joshua Smyth, researchers who found evidence that suggested expressive writing, as they call it, could improve mental health and ease emotional pain.[3] This too got my attention.

Could there be some science in journalling for the soul?

Outrageous Conversations

> Do not be conformed to this world, but be transformed by the renewal of your mind, that by testing you may discern what is the will of God, what is good and acceptable and perfect.
> **Romans 12:2**

Despite struggling with it, I always put an importance on prayer, as I did in studying the Bible. What emerged for me was the combination of the Bible and my soul journal as a key arena, a primary place and practice to renew my mind. As the safety of my journal grew, I began to write my candid thoughts and questions to God more freely. And then… I dared to write down what I heard God was saying to me!

This step was huge. Suddenly I began hearing God in a fresh, new and specific way, all through my journal. In the pages of my journal, I met with the living God.

Almost at the same time, doubts rose in my mind. Could this really be God? A strong, anxious thought came from within:

> *Are you saying that what you write down is on a par with Scripture? Is this really legitimate? It seems outrageous!*

The nature of this particular voice gave it away. I had heard this voice before; it was the voice of the judgmental Pharisee. It was a voice alien to the heart of God.

I grew in confidence, not only that God would speak to me while I was journalling, but also that he gave me the freedom to write down what I thought he was saying to me. I realised it was my birthright as a son of God. I could hear him for myself. I know the Shepherd's voice.

Then over the years, I discovered others like me, who dared to write down what they thought God was saying to them in their journals.

So now, my journalling gained a whole new level of potency. It was more than self-expression, more than emotional processing, more than writing out my prayers; it was a place to encounter God on the page.

However, as I turned my soul to hear his voice, I had to attend to something else as well, which I will come onto in the chapter on *Noise*.

The Rest of This Book

My story, in part, continues over the next few chapters, in *Part 1 - My Journey*, I tell how I struggled with the problem of *Noise* in my life, the distractions and the drivenness that our culture tempts us all with, that has prevented me at times from exploring with God the state of my own soul. Then, in the chapter on *Hearing*, I gave my soul a voice, which led to hearing his. I learned the benefit of slowing down, and more on how science is validating the value of this, as well as settling the problem of my journal's audience.

If you want to begin your soul journalling right now, then skip straight to *Part 2 - Practical Prayer on the Page*. It begins with the chapter on *Starting*. I give you some tips on the tools I use, when I write, and where I write. If the chapter on *Starting* helps you begin a soul journalling routine, *Growing* will help you develop it into a habit, and it may change form. So, as an example, I set out some more of the stages of my personal journey. It is not all positive, as the chapter on *The Perfect Lie* shows. Seeing and naming this lie for what it is disempowers it. The Perfect Lie is universal: all of us are tempted to believe this lie. And there's more. How soul journalling can spill over into the way you live and work, is the subject of the chapter on *Abundance*. And I talk about the *Media* you might consider when soul journalling.

Part 3 - Making Sense of All This, looks at some of the surprising outcomes of soul journalling in *Blessings*. There were some areas that confused me for a while and might be an issue for you too. *Soul* is where I explain what I discovered our soul is, why it differs from our spirit, and why an understanding of the difference between our soul and our spirit matters. Whenever anyone ventures to write anything like this of a personal nature, people can take what the writer says to the extreme, so I include a chapter on *What I am Not Saying*, as well as key references and resources. And finally, *Future* is about how, as part of our journey, soul journalling sets us up for an exciting future, our unique destiny as his child.

In *Part 4 - Materials*, we compare again handwriting versus screen-based journalling and I offer some suggestions about tools that can serve us. This book began, in part, as a case for a return to *Handwriting*, and this chapter covers some of the benefits that are more strongly in evidence in handwriting as opposed to the digital space. This is followed by the chapter on **Digital**. I recognise that handwriting is something many struggle with, having become so accustomed, as most of us have, to the keyboard. That being the case, this chapter offers you some tools to do this, as well as a way to straddle both the analog and digital worlds.

Throughout this book you will find practical *Activations*. These are included to get you started, or to help you move deeper, in your own soul journalling. One of my reviewers said that reviewing the draft made her want to start journalling right away. If you feel that way, simply put this book down and start! So, here's the first one:

Activation

If you can't wait to read the rest of this book, but want to start now, then try this to activate yourself:

✓ Take a few moments to still yourself from hurry, and external noise

✓ Ask Holy Spirit to get involved and journal with you

✓ Using what you normally write with, just write thanks, praise and questions

✓ Now, pay attention to his presence and how it makes you feel. Do you get a surge of excitement, or a deep assurance growing as you write?

✓ Can you feel his weight land on a particular phrase or word?

» If so, pause, and pursue it with him....

~~~~~~

PART 1 - A DISCIPLE'S JOURNEY

I didn't remain with the original format of my journal. It evolved. On reflection, I realise that I have developed my form of soul journal over time progressively through three stages:

1. In the initial stage, I experimented with journalling, recording my thoughts and feelings, moving on to a written prayer.

2. There came that moment on my journey, when I resolved for myself the matter of for whom I was writing, that is, my audience. Also, there was the issue of how I should express myself, my voice. Once I had settled the issues of my journal's audience and my voice, I could move relatively quickly to stage two. Then, over time, I began to write down what God had been saying to me outside of my journal time.

3. Where I am these days is that I am enjoying conversational prayer within the act of journalling.

I now understand that these stages are part of my overall journey as a disciple.

CHAPTER 2

Noise

What are you doing here, Elijah?

There he came to a cave and lodged in it. And behold,
the word of the LORD came to him, and he said
to him, "What are you doing here, Elijah?"
1 Kings 19:9 (ESV)

I became aware of noise. In fact, there was so much noise in my life, so much chatter between my ears, that I found it hard to hear God and to connect with him. So, I can relate to this in the life of Elijah. He had moved powerfully as a prophet, but then there came this external death threat from Jezebel, the powerful demon-worshipping queen of Israel. It provoked in response an internal noise of his own thoughts and fears. He repeats his internal narrative almost word-for-word in verses 10 and 14.

"I have been very jealous for the LORD, the God of hosts. For
the people of Israel have forsaken your covenant, thrown down
your altars, and killed your prophets with the sword, and I,
even I only, am left, and they seek my life, to take it away."

It was his internal script. It was a negative declaration. Elijah had committed this response to memory, rehearsed it, and had become a stronghold in Elijah's thinking. For him, this reading of events had become his belief about events at that time.

And it wasn't true.

It is surprising, then, that God appears to him in a whisper (13) and asks him again, "What are you doing here, Elijah?" Perhaps God was inviting him to reconsider his story.

External and Internal Noise

> Don't let the world squeeze you into its own mould.
> **Part of JB Phillips' Translation of Romans 12:2**

One of the ways the world tries to squeeze me into its own mould is by threats. Jezebel sought to frighten Elijah, and she succeeded. Elijah allowed it to become part of his internal narrative. By the time God called to him, Elijah was in anxious turmoil. External noise had become Elijah's internal noise. He listened to fear, and so it was hard for him to listen to God.

As I write this, there is much uncertainty and anxiety here in the UK about Brexit. The external noise for me comes mainly from media that seeks to gain our attention by fear of the future. I cut myself off from that sort of journalism and keep myself informed in other ways. For me, it's part of guarding my heart.

So, in this chapter, I want to examine the external noise in our lives before we go on to the matter of hearing God.

I often need to remove the noise to break a deceptive script in my thinking. And God wants to help me do that. This too is part of renewing my mind and often I use my soul journal to deal with this.

Weapons of Mass Distraction

Not all external noise appears as a threat; it often comes in a more subtle guise. Consider this episode in the ministry of Jesus:

> But Martha was distracted with much serving. And she went up to him and said, "Lord, do you not care that my sister has left me to serve alone? Tell her to help me."
> But the Lord answered her, "Martha, Martha, you are anxious and troubled about many things, but one thing is necessary. Mary has chosen the good portion, which will not be taken away from her."
> **Luke 10:40-42**

As this passage in Luke reveals, attempting to multi-task to satisfy all that distracts us is not a new phenomenon. Jesus' reply is indicative in two particular phrases he uses here: *anxious and troubled by many things*, and *one thing is needful*. In any moment, only one thing deserves your conscious attention. Do I know what that one thing is for me? Often I forget or I'm confused about that one thing:

"What is on the cinema this week?"

"What am I going to cook tonight?"

"What do I need to get in from the shops?"

"What is this coming into my inbox? Should I answer it now?"

"And what's that ping on my phone?"

I recognised that I was profoundly distracted. I was distracted away from what Stephen Covey calls **The Main Thing**. In his book, *Principle-Centered Leadership*, which interestingly pre-dates much of the technological noise we now experience, Covey majors on a very simple mantra:

The Main Thing is to Keep the Main Thing the Main Thing

I was just not succeeding in this. I had allowed noise, particularly, in my case, communications technology, to drive me. As a result, I felt sometimes that I had the attention of a goldfish.

The Paradox of Speed

A few years ago, Bill Gates wrote a book called, *Business at the Speed of Light*. Behind this title was a very seductive thesis: we can progress faster. This idea resonates with our awareness that the brain is very fast and that we often feel most business systems impede us by slowing us down.

The brain is indeed very fast. Think about this: our cognitive associations are so fast that we can anticipate and recognise a word before the speaker has even finished saying it. And we do this all the time.

Experiment

Try this for an experiment:

- ask a friend person to tell you when they recognise the name of someone you are about to say

- then say a name like 'Harrison Ford'

It is quite likely that your friend will have not just remembered the name but conjured up a mental image before you had even finished saying the name!

However, there is a big difference between the speed of cognition and the optimal speed for focus and assimilation, for deep thinking. Neuroscientists have established that it is the ability to stay on a subject and review it regularly that can change the density and configuration of our neural network. Such thinking can hard-wire our brain and change its shape. This physical shape-changing phenomenon of our brains rehearsing thought-patterns and skills is what scientists call *neuroplasticity*.

Maybe science is catching up with this call for us as disciples to transform our minds, and proving that this process is even reflected at a biological level.

Our Distraction Culture

Here is something I observe almost every day in public places:

> I remember recently sitting in a café, drinking tea and reading a book. I became aware of an elderly couple come and sit on the table next to me. After a short discussion about what they would like to eat, it all fell silent. I glanced over. (Their *silence* distracted me!)
>
> They were both on their smartphones, and this for several minutes, until their meal arrived. Periodically, one of their phones would beep, which I assume meant that a chat message had come from one of their social media networks.

Well, there's nothing remarkable about that, you might think.

That is my point.

Being available to distraction has become, for many of us, part of our accepted social culture. You could call it a distraction culture. I become so used to distraction that I miss it when it is not there. I expect to be diverted. I expect to be entertained. I look forward to the little rush it gives me. I become easily bored. These are signs of a sort of mental addiction

Quite apart from the long-term impacts it could have on our relationships, it has had, in my own case, a significant adverse effect on my creativity and productivity. I wrote "*had*" in that last sentence because I have since taken steps to protect my work from distraction.

Distracted from our Best

Research reveals that the environment of our work matters a great deal.[4] How we protect ourselves when engaging in deep work affects the outcomes of both our own lives and those of the organisations we work within.[5] The alternative, argues Cal Newport, is that we fill our lives and our working days with shallow work.

By allowing ourselves to conform to the distraction culture, we are never likely to achieve our best.

There are particular elements to this distraction culture that are not common knowledge, or least, most people are not particularly concerned about.

The Tyranny of Communications Technology

Charles Hummel coined the phrase *The Tyranny of the Urgent*; it is that Martha lifestyle of always prioritising whatever is urgent, being driven by it, being a slave to it.[6] Now we have a more recent, more subtle manifestation of this: the tyranny of communications technology.

First, there was email. We are so used to email now, but I remember when it first came along, email was a thing of wonder. We could send mail across the world… almost instantly!

Later, many of us woke up to the monster we had allowed it to become. First, emails we received each day became a delight, something we could boast about. It became a measure of our importance. Then, many of us began to tire of this growing burden that began to displace much of our working day. If we were not aware of it, we found we would spend hours of an otherwise-productive day, merely trying to respond to all the emails in our inbox. Clearing our inbox became the productivity target. And who told us that we had to do this? Why do we think this target is so important?

Then the smartphone appeared, another marvel of technology. When I first acquired a smartphone, the App Store seemed to burgeon with new apps every week, and most of them free. I downloaded many. It felt like Christmas!

Before long, I found that the phone interrupted conversations with people in my presence. I was annoyed when other people answered their phones when I was talking with them, but I discovered that I too couldn't resist the same temptation. What a hypocrite I was!

Then messages, by email and social media, began to beep at me. These apps I had downloaded now demanded attention. It was like I had a nest of hungry chicks that would chirp until fed by my attention.

And the quicker I responded, the faster some came back with their replies! I was on a sort of hamster wheel: the faster I satisfied social media through my phone, the faster it made demands on me.

Then it dawned on me that I was using this sort of technology as a sort of instant messaging service. Further, I came to realise that the beep could be considered as *Other People's To-Do List for Me.*[7]

Who told me that I had to organise my life that way? I have never found it in any role description I had been given (not that I'd been given many of those). I had let app notifications drive my agenda too much. It was as though I had this unwritten performance objective, and I wasn't quite sure what it was.

Also, the messaging apps, such as on social media, fragmented my attention. This media seemed to be making me ADHD. I needed to focus, but I found that all too frequently the technology was taking my attention elsewhere.

System 1 and System 2 Thinking

In his book, *Thinking Fast, Thinking Slow*, Nobel Prize-winner and economist, Daniel Kahneman, laid out the distinction between two very different forms of thinking, critical to our decision-making as humans.

System 1 thinking is quick, but shallow, crucial for our survival. For example, as I drive on a motorway, I must allow System 1 thinking to help me avoid threatening situations from the behaviour of other drivers. This kind of thinking keeps us alive.

System 2 thinking, however, is slower, more in-depth. This kind of thinking allows me to meditate, to make better decisions over the longer term. When my wife and I considered moving house from Oxfordshire to Kent, we both did much System 2 thinking. We developed a long-term strategy, thinking through as many of the consequences as we could.

Analysing much decision-making in the finance and business world, Kahneman came to a disturbing conclusion. All too many decisions, driven by the context of urgency, fell into the System 1 category, despite these decisions having large and long-term consequences.

With all this, one outcome seems to be that we have created a culture which encourages System 1 thinking and where time to consider our actions is viewed as a luxury at best, and an annoying hesitation at worst.

And yet ... my journalling provided a place of deep thinking, and an invitation to be powerful and not driven. Looking back, my journal helped me move more into System 2 thinking.

Standing Back from All This

Within this conspiracy of distraction, our work becomes a race, as we consort with the tyranny of communications technology. However, as we recognise what is happening and observe it carefully, it can be the beginning of our recovery and growth. I found seeing all this was my first step towards a cure from this addiction.

And I discovered that it was from my soul journal, that I became more aware of all this. Soul journalling began to help me notice the noise and my own handling of it. Perhaps there was something deeper going on as well. My identity was shifting from being a victim who was constantly driven by other forces to that of a son of my heavenly Father, who was invited to explore my freedom as his son.

So, I began to rein myself in. There were some immediate practical steps I could take.

For example, now I delete apps that I have not used for some time; I have worked out how to put my phone into airplane mode, set a timer, and to do this regularly through the day. As a consequence, I am moving to a more conscious and minimalist use of apps. I realise that the cumulative effect of all this makes me more focused and productive. I now use apps as a conscious choice, and not let them use me. I unsubscribe from lists more easily, and delete apps regularly. But part of this self-conscious assertion in my daily habits came through standing back and writing about it reflectively in my journal.

In one sense, all this distraction from apps and communications technology is somewhat trivial. However, it creates within us an internal proclivity that can hinder our ability to make some fairly important, sometimes strategic decisions.

The Strategic Moment

One of my favourite passages in *The Lord of the Rings* trilogy of books- *not* the movies - illustrates vividly how sometimes, reflecting deeply in the face of urgency is the wise thing to do.

At the end of the first book, Aragorn, is the leader of the Fellowship of the Ring, a small band who are commissioned to escort and guard Frodo, the Ringbearer on a perilous mission. At the beginning of Book Two, he now appears to see his mission fall apart before his eyes. Because of a surprise ambush, a key member of his team is slain, valiantly but vainly protecting two others, who are both now captured by the marauding band of Orcs.

And it gets worse for Aragorn. He discovers that Frodo, the Ringbearer, is also missing, along with Sam, Frodo's servant, and one of the boats, apparently having left in the opposite direction, across the river.

Aragorn is having a bad day.

What should he do? The remaining members of the Fellowship spend a precious half hour giving their dead friend, Boromir, a river burial, and time is ticking away. It is urgent! Should Aragorn and the two remaining members of the Fellowship pursue Frodo and Sam to protect the Ringbearer? Isn't this, after all, the Main Thing of their mission? Or instead, should he seek to rescue the other two from the Orcs?

Peter Jackson's first movie of Tolkien's Fellowship of the Ring finishes just before this little gem. The second movie in the series – The Two Towers – skips it altogether! The screenplay writer, no doubt, looked at the story through a 21st century, entertainment lens, a view that can only appreciate the chaotic, System 1 decisions, the fast-paced and more obviously magical.

But in the book, there is this portrayal of timeless wisdom, an object lesson in using System 2 thinking, in what I would call the Strategic Moment. To be sure, the situation requires urgent action, but it had to be strategic. If Aragorn makes the wrong call, then the consequences could be dire.

'Let me think!' said Aragorn. 'And now may I make a right choice, and change the evil fate of this unhappy day!' He stood silent for a moment. 'I will follow the Orcs ... *My heart speaks clearly at last*: [emphasis mine] the fate of the Bearer is in my hands no longer. The Company has played its part...'

For me this story illustrates several qualities of System 2 thinking in a crisis:

1. **Aragorn pauses**. Despite the pressing urgency of the moment, Aragorn actually does something counter-intuitive: he slows down. The enemy cavalry may almost be upon the archers, but they hold their arrows for the right moment. What is crucial is that the aim is sure.

2. **He faces reality**. This is not the time for indulging in denial or retreating into self-pity. Aragorn doesn't bleat, *This can't be happening!* (that all-too-popular idiom these days). Nor should he start to take out his frustration on those comrades who happened to be around.

   No, he calmly faces the situation as it really presents itself. As Max De Pree once said, "A leader defines reality."

   Neither is this the time for grieving. As William Durant, founder of General Motors, once said, "Forget past mistakes. Forget failures. Forget everything except what you're going to do now and do it."

3. **He gives the situation his total attention**. A strategic moment is a mission-critical moment. This is not the time for being distracted. Mental focus is one of the critical disciplines of System 2 thinking.

4. **He searches his head and his heart**. As Spencer Johnson has argued, we make better decisions when our head and our heart agree.[8] We make better decisions that are congruent with our value systems and passion as well as making rational, logical sense.

5. **He releases himself from what he cannot do and focuses on what he can**. Strategic decisions are as much about saying *No* to poor options as saying *Yes* to others. At times we can influence more than at other times; that's just accepting reality.

A real source of unhelpful stress is to get frustrated and angry. We tell ourselves that we don't have as much influence today as yesterday, that some people around us aren't as cooperative or as available today as yesterday, that key people don't seem to be as responsive to us as they have been in the past, and *It's not fair!* We can't afford the luxury of a pity-party. We need to assess the situation as it really is now.

6.   **He is prepared to redefine the Mission.** Aragorn was to escort the Ringbearer to Mordor, but he reflects deeply enough to make even this mission statement negotiable. He identifies the real critical success factor of his mission: to protect as many of his party as he can. What is not negotiable is his value of protecting those whom he can defend. Reflection helps him distinguish values and practice. We need to stay connected with the deepest purposes and reasons in our lives, that we are here by the grace of God to seek first his Kingdom and its righteousness. Out of this, we can give an authentic direction to our lives.

7.   **He takes positive action.** This was not the time, though, for Aragorn to express paralysis by analysis. As a leader, he had a leaning to action. We have done all of the above, but unless we identify and act upon a positive, practical response to the Strategic moment, we will have failed. Consider the question, 'What practical steps can I take now, to model and reinforce this new strategic direction?' Follow through a decision with an immediate step towards it.

I am always fascinated by how people respond in the crucible of a crisis. These are not just strategic moments for whatever we are trying to achieve, but they are also defining moments for the development of character.

I believe that one of the reasons why I can gain so much benefit from soul journalling, particularly handwritten, is because it slows me down to reflect and mull over a subject. Journalling de-complexes my thinking, and perhaps my life as well.

Journalling develops my ability to focus. When I soul journal, I give my focus muscles a workout and build them over time.

You can build your focus too.

So next time you have a crisis, and everyone is clamouring for an urgent remedy, press the pause button ...

.... and have the courage to wait ...

... until your heart speaks clearly.

Activation

✓   Find a time and/or somewhere you can withdraw

Prayerfully consider:

✓   What are the noises which distract you from drawing nearer to God and engaging in meaningful thinking?

✓   Ask Holy Spirit to bring them to mind so that you can list them.

✓   Now look at your list. Are these noises or distractions internal (eg worry) or external (eg social media)?

✓   What practical steps can you take to

»   reduce the noise,

»   create space for your own thoughts and

»   for you to hear God speak?

Write these down.

Calming the Noise

As we have already noted, noise comes from within and without. Whatever the source of my noise, I noticed that the practice of being with God, of dwelling in his presence, began to deal with it.

Internal noise can be seen for what it really is. Often listening to that internal narrative and writing it down starts to calm it.

External noise — the distractions, fragmentation and the urges of the urgent, can also be dealt with by withdrawing, as Jesus did, into the wilderness. My testimony is that soul journalling can become a prime means of doing this without finding a natural wilderness. There is no literal wilderness near my home in Kent anyway; it's the garden of England! However, I have made a lonely place and time for myself in my practice of soul journalling.

I have a choice. I am not a victim. I can allow myself to be carried along by noise and find that the external noise can be toxic. It can be believed and owned by me. If I make it my own, it becomes my internal noise. For example, I can hear a view on the news media presented as a serious threat, and I can believe and focus on it; and it becomes my internal anxiety. It becomes part of my internal noise.

Yet, there is no fear in heaven. Jesus commanded his disciples several times not to fear. Fear, in particular, is the internal noise that I am called upon to repent from by trusting in a God greater than my fear. And so are you.

If I can calm the internal chatter, I have a better chance of hearing. But to whom am I listening? How can I be sure that voice is God's? We will look at that next.

CHAPTER 3

Hearing

But when he came to himself...

But he who enters by the door is the shepherd of the sheep. To him the gatekeeper opens. The sheep hear his voice, and he calls his own sheep by name and leads them out. When he has brought out all his own, he goes before them, and the sheep follow him, for they know his voice...I am the good shepherd. The good shepherd lays down his life for the sheep.
John 10:2-4; 11

See what kind of love the Father has given to us, that we should be called children of God: and so we are. The reason why the world does not know us is that it did not know him.
1 John 3:1

One of the outstanding discoveries for me was that the God of this universe chose to adopt me as his child. And he speaks to his children. It is the birthright of all of us born of the Spirit. We all can and should hear him.

More than that, I came to realise that his Holy Spirit dwelt in me. His own thoughts interact with mine. This is where we need to understand what is his kind of thought and what is not. Vicky Schulz tells me:

> An example for us is our daughter – away at college. She regularly calls or messages us with her thoughts, plans and ideas. We cheer her on, ask her questions and offer advice or a gentle steer when appropriate. As parents, we love being involved in her process.

So, why do we think it would be otherwise with our heavenly Father? Can we all hear him? Yes, we can.

In a Desolate Place

> And rising very early in the morning, while it was still dark, he departed and went out to a desolate place, and there he prayed. And Simon and those who were with him searched for him, and they found him and said to him, "Everyone is looking for you." And he said to them, "Let us go on to the next towns, that I may preach there also, for that is why I came out."
> **Mark 1:35-38 (ESV)**

Unlike Elijah, Jesus sought a desolate place, free from the agendas, urgencies and the distractions of others, to hear his Father. And he was ready with a new direction when Simon and the others found him. Important business had been done when Jesus was alone with the Father in prayer. He had clarified with his Father his Main Thing and, perhaps, his next step.

As I have described, journalling became for me a purposeful withdrawing from engagement with the world. It is withdrawing to engage with my heavenly Father. I begin to process my own internal thoughts, beliefs, feelings, and expectations. In this withdrawing, the external noise is lowered, if not absent altogether, and I can hear Father much more clearly. It's as if heaven turns down the volume control.

Listening to my Soul

> I have hidden your word in my heart that I might not sin against you.
> **Psalm 119:11**

The ancients believed meditation to be a vital spiritual discipline. They regarded it as a self-directed means of personal transformation.

I began soul journalling because I found prayer difficult, but I've continued with it because …

Well, there are many reasons, some of which I will touch on later. But one of the main reasons is that it is a habit that helps keep my thoughts on message, on his message. It helps me pay attention.

The more I practice this kind of journalling, the more I grow in self-awareness. As with Elijah, I had not appreciated how a lot of the internal noise in my head was my own thoughts and feelings being repeated over and over again. It seemed that some of these thoughts and emotions simply wanted the courtesy of being acknowledged.

Writing down those thoughts and feelings were the beginning of that acknowledgement. As I started to listen to my own soul, it was as if it was satisfied. I could then move on.

Improved Self-Awareness

> But when he came to himself, he said, 'How many of my father's hired servants have more than enough bread, but I perish here with hunger! I will arise and go to my father, and I will say to him, "Father, I have sinned against heaven and before you. I am no longer worthy to be called your son. Treat me as one of your hired servants."'
> **Luke 15:17-19**

It was after I had established soul journalling as a key habit in my life that I began to research good self-leadership, that led to my writing my earlier book, *Leading Yourself: Succeeding from the Inside Out*. It was during that research that it became clearer to me how important this matter of self-awareness was to living life more fully.

This kind of self-awareness is not the same as self-regarding or being proud in an egotistical way. Healthy self-awareness is being able to read my one soul, moment-by-moment, particularly that emotional part of myself. When someone is described as "flying off the handle," with uncontrollable anger, then it might indicate that they need to grow in self-awareness, in the ability to track their emotions, to take their own emotional temperature. In the research into emotional intelligence (EQ), this kind of self-awareness is the bedrock of self-management. And EQ seems to be a key discriminator over the long-term as to how much someone will achieve in life. Moreover, one of the fruits of the Spirit is self-control.

In his remarkable autobiography, *Man's Search for Meaning*, Viktor Frankl describes at one point being tortured in Auschwitz.[9] His last freedom, as he described it, was that gap between action — what his torturer did — and his mental and emotional reaction. He came to believe that for every action of external circumstances upon his life, Frankl had a choice as to how he would react. Even in this extreme situation, he discovered freedom through exercising the choice in that gap between the actions on him and his reaction to them. However, it required great self-awareness.

The cure from the sorts of distraction I described earlier begins with self-awareness. I come to terms with the fact that I am all too easily distracted from my best work. I observe it, and describe it before the Lord in my journal.

Researchers have identified self-awareness as the foundation of EQ; this ability to think about our thinking, to appraise our own thought processes critically. As studies have shown, the self-aware are more self-possessed … and more successful. They are better able to delay gratification and set to work. It is the ability to examine our own thought processes. It is a faculty closely associated with people who excel in their field, whom I call the Positive Outliers. This self-clarity removes much noise and distraction helping us to focus and do our best work.

> Everthing can be taken from a man but one thing: the last of human freedoms -- to choose one's attitude in any given set of circumstances, to choose one's own way.
> **Viktor Frankl**

Then with self-awareness, I can come to the conclusion that I have a choice. Victims don't have a choice. Slaves don't have a choice. I choose not to be a victim nor a slave; these are not my identity. I can choose.

I am always concerned when clients say, "I can't turn my phone off for periods during the day." Unless they are in some critical support function, yes they can. So can I. Freedom begins when I admit that I have a choice.

I can choose consciously to limit communications applications, particularly in those moments when I journal. Some writers have chosen to work on disconnected, or unconnected computers.

As a disciple, growing in self-awareness is for me growing in God's image. Self-awareness is a higher-order human capacity, not shared in the animal kingdom. With self-awareness, I can stand outside myself and observe my own soul. This led the prodigal to repent.

And it led me to repent as well. Without this ability to be self-aware, I could not admit that I had sinned. Without self-awareness, we would all live as sociopaths, living purely from self-interest.

Slowing Down

I want it all, and I want it now.
Songwriters: **Brian May, Freddie Mercury, John Deacon, Michie Nakatani, Roger Taylor**

However, I found that paying attention required a different pace. It seems that self-awareness happens best when I am not rushed.

Writing, particularly handwriting, has slowed me down enough so that, without realising it, I learned, as all persistent meditators do, that returning to the same themes is OK; even beneficial.

This makes no sense at all to the restless, who are always searching for new data, new facts, new information. They find themselves demanding new answers now. They might react: *Yeah! Yeah! 'been there, done that. Let's move on! Give me something new!* Maybe we all recognise something of that in ourselves, where there have been times when we too have been restless and impatient to press into something new.

Blessed is the man
who walks not in the counsel of the wicked,
nor stands in the way of sinners,
nor sits in the seat of scoffers;
but his delight is in the law of the LORD,
and on his law he meditates day and night.
He is like a tree planted by streams of water
that yields its fruit in its season,
and its leaf does not wither.
In all that he does, he prospers.
Psalm 1:1-3

For true personal transformation, I must mull over profound truths again and again. I need to shift gears. In my experience, Holy Spirit never tires of leading me back over old ground again and again. For him, this seems to be the progress he wants to take me through, even though I cannot see it in myself. This then becomes a matter of faith; trusting him with the process.

If you can worry, you can meditate.
John Ortberg

However, if I continue with the mental equivalent of fast food then little penetrates, little goes deep. There is no nourishment. My soul requires me to slow down and digest, to go deep into subjects and return to them again and again from different angles. Writing down my thoughts can help me do just that.

As I noted in the previous chapter, System 2 thinking is likely to be slower. As I write reflectively, I rediscover the ability of deep thought.

Neuroscience is Noticing

A man is what he thinks about all day long.
Ralph Waldo Emerson

Science is now identifying how intentional meditation like this seems to make an impact. The self-directing neuroplasticity of the human brain is such that frequently used mental pathways — synaptic traces through the neocortex — quite literally these repeated thoughts change the shape of our brains. More than that, they seem to correlate with who we think we are.[10] In plain terms, as Emerson wrote some 150 years ago, you become what you think about all the time. There is some correlation between people who meditate and a higher density of synapses in the prefrontal cortex.

Might this be a physical expression of the transformation to which Romans 12:2 refers?

Surprise in Schipol

For a while, I would write my journal in an A5 notebook. One time, I was travelling back from the Netherlands and was returning to the UK. I had an hour or two to spare in Schipol Airport without anything to read. Hesitantly, I opened my journal, which was nearly full from about nine months' worth of entries. I was hesitant because I had expected to read a depressing account of a repeated cycle of failure and struggle. Up to that time, I would write in my journal but hardly ever read each day's entry afterwards.

Instead, what I found amazed me: it was a progressive and positive pattern in my internal life that I would not have discovered otherwise. It surprised me. Holy Spirit had evidently been moving me forward, growing me, and I had not appreciated it.

This is not a regular experience in my journalling. Usually, I do not re-read previous days' entries, unless I feel prompted by Holy Spirit to do so.

As I have already said, I realised that it is not the content of the soul journal that is so valuable to me so much as the ***process*** of writing it, of getting my thoughts and feelings down on paper. Yet, there have been significant occasions, such as at Schipol, where Holy Spirit has used past journals to encourage me.

These experiences, though, shifted something in my thinking. Yes, it is the process of writing that is most valuable, but what I do write can have value lasting far longer than when I wrote it originally — even if I never re-read it. If meditation is part of mind renewal, then writing can be an expression of such meditation. Therefore, I regard writing another day's entry as creating a renewal asset, something that has spiritual value. This, in turn, has motivated me to keep going and journal.

What We Value Grows

> "For it will be like a man going on a journey, who called his servants and entrusted to them his property... He also who had received the one talent came forward, saying, 'Master, I knew you to be a hard man, reaping where you did not sow, and gathering where you scattered no seed, so I was afraid, and I went and hid your talent in the ground.'"
>
> **Matthew 25:14, 24-25**

I have learned an important dynamic in the Kingdom of God, which is this: what I value, grows. Take, for example, prophecies. I have received a number of prophecies. If I value them, I record them, pray over them, declare them over myself, position myself to be ready for them to happen, return to them again later, and perhaps even taking a conscious step towards their fulfilment. This expression of valuing appears to invite God to do more in my life. If I neglect a particular area of what Holy Spirit gives me, it will atrophy and die. So, what I do with what I have been given matters. It's my part in being his disciple. I must steward these things.

So, if I value hearing God, then why would I not take steps to make listening to God more possible? For me, this has involved my soul journal as a key practice in that process of stewarding what God has given me.

Hearing: A Summary

So, here's a summary of what I was beginning to realise:

- The gospels reveal that Jesus regularly withdrew to lonely places to pray. I live better if I do the same.

- Soul journalling became a way for me of withdrawing from the world to be with Father.

- Journalling gave my soul a voice, at the heart level.

- Journalling can help me grow in self-awareness, a critical faculty to living well. My self-awareness is as much about noticing my internal emotional and cognitive narratives as it about to how I come over to others in social settings.

- In turn, this increased self-awareness helped me grow in emotional intelligence, moving me from a victim mindset to one where I can be aware of making powerful choices.

- Journalling, particularly the handwritten form, slows me down (a good thing), and engages me in System 2 thinking.

- Neuroscience is agreeing with what I realise is going on in my soul. There is now emerging evidence that frequent practice of such techniques gives physical expression in my brain.

- What I value grows. If I value hearing Him, my ability to hear God grows.

But, if you have never journalled before, how do you start?

This is what I deal with next, in Part 2.

PART 2- PRACTICAL PRAYER
ON THE PAGE

Despite touching on some of this in the activations, here I cover some of the more practical elements of getting started, growing a soul journalling habit and thoughts on how we can use different media.

Without being too prescriptive, I want to give you a few tips, lessons I have learned along the way.

CHAPTER 4
Starting

"It is like a grain of mustard seed..."

S o, how do you get started with soul journalling? I find that when I am starting to learn any new routine, developing any new habit or skill, it helps if I follow the advice I am given fairly closely for the first ten days or so. By then, I usually have some idea as to where I might like to adapt that advice for my own situation and personal style.

As you go on, you will sense God's leading in a particular ways; it is part of your adventure as a disciple. If you have already had some experience with journalling over some time, take the following advice lightly and tailor it to your own preferences. Even so, you are likely to gain some fresh practical insights.

> And he said, "With what can we compare the kingdom of God, or what parable shall we use for it? It is like a grain of mustard seed, which, when sown on the ground, is the smallest of all the seeds on earth, yet when it is sown it grows up and becomes larger than all the garden plants and puts out large branches, so that the birds of the air can make nests in its shade."
> **Mark 4:30-32**

In the parable of the mustard seed, Jesus teaches an important Kingdom dynamic about growth. If soul journalling becomes anything of value for you, it will aid the growth of the Kingdom within you and around you. As you begin, what you write might contain that small seed — in fact, it probably will. As you practice, that which is of heaven in what you write will germinate in the soil of your soul. When the practice has developed roots in you deep enough, it will make an appearance above the surface of your soul; it has now become a habit. Later it will bear more fruit.

In his book, **Atomic Habits**, James Clear argues that when developing any new routine, starting small is the best way by far.[11] In fact, the subtitle of his book is:

Tiny Changes, Remarkable Results.

He invites people to consider aiming for a one per cent improvement each day. Over a few days, a one per cent improvement is negligible, but over a year the cumulative effect can be tremendous.

Some Ways of Beginning

Down through the centuries, there have been certain practices that help the disciple write. Here are a few of them.

Start Small

Start small and build your soul journalling habit over time.

Beginning any new routine that you want to become a habit can be difficult. There are some techniques, though, that can help us all establish a good new habit. For example, you can make it easy for yourself by having the materials to hand in the place where you will journal. If you are trying to find your stationery when you want to use them, it will deter you.

> When I returned to the routine of going to the gym, I began by setting out my clothes and trainers. I was even prepared to put on my trainers as the next step, and maybe not yet go to the gym. Just putting on the trainers was progress; in fact, I never stopped there. Very soon, gym sessions became routine.

Each day you can try to increase the amount you write or the time you spend writing until you either fill the page or hit a word-count target, or reach about 30 minutes. Again, this is not a hard-and-fast rule; just a guide.

So, make it easy for yourself to start. So, how do you start small? It might be a sentence, or writing for no more than two minutes; starting small for you might involve scheduling a particular time of the day in your diary for this.

Some Starter Tools

Here are some suggestions for your starter tools. This list is deliberately minimal. I will discuss adding to it later.

For handwriting, I recommend the stationery you are most comfortable with. For example:

- A writing pad or exercise book. For now, it is better if you use a notebook exclusively for your soul journal. Choose something around A5 size. The page size is not too daunting, but it gives you some freedom.

- If you have a favourite pen or pencil, use that. If you don't yet have a favourite, try a gel pen. Go for something that gives you less friction as you write on the page.

For typing:

- Use the app or software with which you already familiar; for many people, this could be Microsoft Word, for example.

- Also, if the software has a fullscreen mode, that is, without anything else showing on the screen, use it.

- Switch off any notifications on the device you are using, such as:
    - » Email alerts
    - » Social media alerts
    - » Alarms
    - » Call alerts or rings.

Tip: An easy way to do this is simply to switch a portable device like a tablet or phone to **airplane mode** while you are journalling.

Note that my handwriting list is shorter. This speaks volumes about the simplicity of handwriting as opposed to the multiple potential distractions that await us in the digital space. I share more thoughts on this in Part 4 - *Materials*.

Two Key Dimensions

> But when you pray, go into your room and shut the
> door and pray to your Father who is in secret. And
> your Father who sees in secret will reward you.
>
> Matthew 6:6

There are two salient elements in this text: ***audience*** and ***place***. Place reinforces who the audience really is. As I mentioned earlier, Jesus taught this at a time when ostentatious religious practice, such as praying, was particularly flagrant. Religious leaders of his day would find human audiences, the attention of others, so that they could demonstrate their religiosity in public. It was all a performance for others to applaud.

The Secret Place

This was never the case with Jesus. He regularly withdrew to lonely places, places where he was alone with Abba, places where there was no other social interaction. In fact, at one time, his closest disciples even had to ask him how to pray. This was unusual, since the tradition of disciples was to repeat what they heard their rabbi praying.

In 2018, my wife and I travelled to Israel with a group led by Mark Hendley. I was not prepared for the Judean wilderness. I had seen deserts in other parts of the world, in Arabia, in the Americas, but nothing compared with this. It was utterly barren and hostile. Mark told me that it is called a pocket desert because you can walk out of it.

And this was the place the Holy Spirit chose to lead Jesus into for forty days after his baptism!

People who pray in public to impress other people, perhaps succeed; some people may be impressed. But that is the entire benefit of the exercise: the brief, passing admiration, perhaps, of their human audience.

Maybe that is a significant reason why my soul journal is so powerful for me. Abba rewards me when it's just him and me. Abba and I have business to do together, and I have his treasures to uncover.

Your Audience Who is in Secret

One particular area I found somewhat distracting early on in my soul journalling was in deciding for whom was I writing. *Who is my audience?* What if someone stumbled upon my journal? What if I was to show this to someone? I taught regularly at my church at that time, so I kept thinking, *These would make good preaching notes.*

This matter settled itself over time; it became irrelevant. What I came to realise is that with soul journalling, the primary audience is me…. and God. No one else is involved, so no one else, for the moment, matters.

If you journal with the intent that you will show it to others, then it is no longer reflective writing, no longer soul journalling. You need to settle this for yourself: write only for you and God.

However, that is not to say that you may be prompted by the Lord to re-read and share something with others afterwards. This often happens with me.

> At one time, I journaled about a setback in my business. At the time I wrote it for myself and before the Lord. That was my audience. However, I later realised that what I had written was so relevant to a conference that I would speak at later in the week. I quoted the text to the audience.

That is OK. At the time, I wrote reflectively, personally, but only afterwards did it emerge that what I had journalled in private had a lot of relevance for this conference. It was my original and prime motive that mattered. If others got blessed later, that was a bonus.

The principle is: settle it in your mind that, *at the time of writing*, you are only writing for you and God. Nobody else will see it. It is for you. Then you will find you can settle into writing for that audience quite easily.

And one of the reasons that the format of your journalling really does not matter is because your audience is only you and God, and He understands what you have put down, however scrambled, untidy and chaotic it may appear.

Creating the Write Environment

So, **where** you write is important. As I have stressed in the chapter on **Noise**, be aware that one of the major inhibitors to soul journalling can be distractions. We can be easily distracted or even discouraged if we do not have the right materials to hand. The materials and the medium of our writing can irritate and annoy us. They become impediments to the free flow of writing.

Some people value a silent place of solitude. Withdrawing into that place can become like a physical act of worship. It becomes a holy place for them.

Sometimes, the ambient noise in a place is a blessing. If it is the right kind of noise, it can help us to flow in our journalling. For example, have you ever wondered why it is sometimes easier to work in a busy coffee shop? Many find that a local café is their best place for uninterrupted journalling.[12] There can be multiple reasons, but a major one is, I think, it takes us away from the usual distractions of our workplace or home.

Now, doesn't writing in a public place seem at odds with the secret place Jesus teaches us to find? It depends on where you are most accessible to others. The same Jesus who taught about the secret place was also regularly observed by his disciples praying. For example, in Luke 11:1 it reads:

> Now Jesus was praying in a certain place, and when he had finished, one of his disciples said to him, "Lord, teach us to pray, as John taught his disciples."

And he did. By that time, I imagine among his closest disciples, Jesus had established boundaries around his prayer that allowed its protection, even when he was still physically near them.

Another key to creating the best environment is to reduce the impediments to focus. Most people's personal workspace is cluttered with post-it notes, pinging social media comments, and so on.

Your Voice

Also, when I first started journalling, the voice I used when I wrote would trouble me a lot. Was it the correct style for journalling?

I discovered that finding my voice was rather like staying upright on a bicycle. When I first learned to cycle, quite late in my boyhood —I was about seven years old! — I discovered I was staying upright merely by trying to steer the bike. As soon as I focused elsewhere, cycling became easier. In the same way, I found my voice by focusing on other things, like the content of what I was trying to express.

This became for me one of the delights of practice, of forming a journalling habit. I discovered my voice; it *emerged.*

So, my recommendation is not to focus on finding your voice. Instead, focus on your reflections, on hearing the Spirit. Your voice will come.

When to Write

It's 8:02 in the evening. That's an unusual time for me to write. I always feel I do my best work in the mornings.

A client of mine works long days as a medical practitioner. She needs to get out the door early to be at work on time in the morning. Morning journalling would not work for her, whereas it is my best time before the world comes to me. She finds that her best time is in the evening.

It may be different for you. So find *your* best time.

There is the common myth that one is either a morning person, who is most productive when fresh in the morning or else is an evening person, who comes alive after dark. I'm always testing this theory by asking people.

The other day, a friend of mine told me that he felt he had changed his preferences about when was the ideal time of day for him to journal, as he grew older. He is now finding that the mornings are the best time for him. We agreed that he may be experiencing it as such now as he becomes older and has less energy.

Perhaps it is only partly energy; maybe it has as much to do with protected time. Right now, for example, it is not an ideal journalling time for me. I have two distractions: my laptop is on next to me, and through the doorway of my study I can hear the washing machine throbbing.

Whatever the time of day you choose to journal, it is best to stick to it, at least until you form a journalling habit. Routine builds a habit, which in turn yields benefit.

"Yesterday"

Bill Hybels recommends beginning with the word *Yesterday*. This leads us into reflecting on what happened to us the day before, what we felt, how we reacted, and why we reacted in that way. Bill is definitely someone who rises early and retires early, so this works well for him. His daily cycle is to look back overnight to the day before.

If you prefer to write in the evening, then use the Hebraic day, which begins at sunset, and look at the day just ending as the previous day.

Hybels also recommends writing a prayer on the opposite page. I structured it this way: first, I wrote no more than a few sentences with thanks, and then with praise. This is a biblical sequence, thanks followed by praise, as found in Psalm 100:

> Enter his gates with thanksgiving, and his courts with praise!
> **Psalm 100:4**

As this Psalm indicates, a grateful heart naturally leads us into worship. So, I began with thanksgiving.

Then I would move into petitions for others and then requests for myself. While I don't advise this is where you stay in your soul journal, it was a starter format for me that I found very helpful.

Early Analog Alternatives

Even at this early stage, though, cursive handwriting might still be a barrier. My recommendation is to try handwriting for about five days. If you are still struggling with it, then try something different.

Sasha Caridia, has developed her own form of sketch-noting or mind mapping her journal. She has kindly sent me some photos of these. Here's one example:

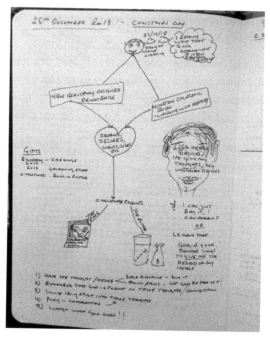

As you can see, she prefers diagrams and pictures over handwriting in prose. She is using a more visual form of journalling that has merit in getting the topics of her soul down on paper. The main thing is to get your thoughts down. The format doesn't matter.

Connecting with the joy of soul journalling

When journalling, we are more likely to connect early on with the joy of soul journalling by remembering the following:

1. Accepting that writing in a soul journal is deep work, and so we need to focus.

2. Creating a ritual of soul journalling at a particular time of the day.

3. Disconnecting. That means going offline, muting alerts, closing down other apps, clearing your desk of clutter. Think of this as unplugging *yourself*.

4. Using materials that give you joy. If you are handwriting, use good stationery. This will take you a long way. I have come to like particular sorts of stationery. I now enjoy writing; it is a pleasure. With the right stationery, it is as if the pen just flows.

    If you are writing on a digital device, use your favourite or preferred writing app.

Activation

- Have your tools to hand

- Choose your favourite, protected time and space

- Begin with the word "Yesterday"

- Write one sentence today, and then one sentence more than you did yesterday. Each day, build this up until you can write a page. Or write for one minute more than you did yesterday

- Add a sentence on the opposite page of:

  » What I am thankful for is …

  » Praise

  » Request for others

  » Request for yourself

- Agree that you write for yourself and for God; that is your audience.

- Experiment with place and time. Find the best place for you to journal, in secret, free from distractions, and find when in the day you can journal most freely.

Also:

- Mind Map using an unusual word which strikes you as you write it down. You could even use the word PRAYER as a starting point, as the central word in your Mind Map.

CHAPTER 5
Growing

"Take a large tablet..."

G etting started in the soul journalling routine is one thing, establishing it as a habit is quite another. How do you develop soul journalling into a habit? When it becomes a habit, something else can happen: it becomes a precious medium for a two-way conversation with the living God.

Increasing my borders

Then the LORD said to me, "Take a large tablet and write on it in common characters, 'Belonging to Hajer-shalal-hash-baz.'"
Isaiah 8:1

One aspect that seems to affect my flow in writing is the size of the portal I write on. Research in the 1980s into the productivity of computer programmers revealed that the size of their desk space was a critical indicator of their productivity.[13] At that time, computer programmers first coded on paper and only then entered their code on an expensive time-shared mainframe computer. So, their working desk space was their portal. As we journal, the area within which we write is our portal.

When I have journaled on a smartphone, I was quite constrained by such a small portal, its screen size. I find that a smartphone screen is sufficient for me to send someone a short text or to make a call, but I struggle to write an entry of any significant size on my phone.[14]

Yes, I know; smartphones *do* have word processors; yes, I can use them to write; but are they the best devices for this purpose? I don't think so.

When I do use my phone in this way, I wonder whether I have sacrificed deep expression for convenience? There is something about seeing a larger canvas that helps creative expression. I can see the whole as well as the details. Being able to journal on a larger screen can help.

This principle also holds true in the analog world. For example, I usually carry a pocket notebook and a gel pen with me; the notebook is small enough for my back pocket. This kind of stationery is great for jotting down short notes. But when writing anything longer, I prefer an A5 or A4 notebook.

This is even more compelling when using non-linear note-making techniques, such as Mind Mapping. I was once commissioned through Tony Buzan's organisation to draw mind maps for a publication on high school exams in Double Science.[15] My preferred portal for that project was not A4 but the larger landscape A3 sketch pads.

The larger the portal or canvas, the larger the degree of freedom for the writer. This is true for journalling as well as for drawing or for writing bug-free software.

So, as well as choosing your medium, consider the size of your portal.

S.O.A.P.

Some structure is helpful, such as the sequence of a journal entry. It is not essential to follow the structure, but it removes other distractions, that can stall or interrupt the flow. For example, questions we raise such as, What should I cover? What should I start writing about? What should I write next?

As I became more practised, the structure of my journalling changed. After a while, I began to move on from the one offered by Bill Hybels. I adopted one more grounded in the Scriptures. I started using a daily journalling framework called SOAP journalling that I came across years ago, and then through my friends, Mark Appleyard and Rob Schulz.[16]

SOAP is an acronym:

✓   **S** is for **Scripture**. First, write out a text.

For example, over the last couple of years, I have been working my way through whole books of the Bible: John, Philippians, Nehemiah, Galatians, now Luke. I have also read one chapter a day in Proverbs over a month. I wrote down the verse or verses that stood out to me in that day's chapter.

As you write, this is part of your meditation on that text, which leads on to the next section of SOAP.

✓   **O** is for **Observation**. Write down what you notice about that text. Often, this will call to mind another verse, which I also write down. You will find that the Holy Spirit invariably brings something fresh, even to verses that are very familiar to you. Again, it is the process of responding and writing out the Scripture text that allows you to hear God more clearly.

✓   **A** stands for **Application**. Here, you think about what the response in your own life should be.

I am amazed by how the sequence of following Luke's gospel is so relevant to what is happening in my life at the moment. How does God do that?

And finally,

✓   **P** is for **Prayer**. This is where you respond directly to God in writing. This is where exciting things happen; like a written conversation with the Almighty!

Mark Appleyard recommends one additional step, which he maintains is the most important one:

    ✓   A **Topic Index**. Keep a few pages blank at the beginning when starting a new journal. When an entry is finished, give your entry a title. Then, put that title on the list in the first few pages against the date. This allows you to see a pattern over a week or month or longer in your journal.

        I do this somewhat differently now, which I will cover later, both in the chapter on *Abundance* and further in my use of Evernote in chapter 8 on *Media*.

Intimacy with God

> And there has not arisen a prophet since in Israel like
> Moses, whom the LORD knew face to face,
> **Deuteronomy 34:10**

Intimacy with God is an imperative for all disciples; we are commanded to love God, not merely obey him. And this intimacy with him is an often-unexplored delight, waiting for each of us.

The benefit of intimacy with God as you write is vast. When you write your prayers, you are likely to find your soul journal has particular value in helping you to hear God better. You find that you write aware that your prayer is part of an ongoing dialogue with him. And more than that, you begin to write down what you think he is saying to you. You have conversations with him in your journal! Now, this gets exciting.

Moses was known as a man with whom God spoke face to face. As I re-read my journal entries, I realise that it is enabling me, in a some measure, to do that as well.

Strengthened by Joy

You make known to me the path of life;
in your presence there is fullness of joy;
at your right hand are pleasures forevermore.
Psalm 16:11

Joy is the serious business of heaven.
CS Lewis

As we have considered, we become writers by writing. We become disciples by watching and following; that is, talking with, following and obeying our Rabbi, our Lord. And if there is no joy in the process, something is wrong. The religious spirit always seeks to suck the joy out of intimacy with God.

Habits are established from routines and they are more likely to become habits if there is also some positive payback, some reward. So it is crucial for all of us that we connect with the joy of the soul journal early enough. That the Lord meets me in my soul journal is a tremendous gift. I would not trade it for anything.

Activation

As you practice, you will get better. Here are some suggestions for you along the way:

- ✓ Write something every day

- ✓ Occasionally, as you are prompted to, encourage yourself by re-reading your journals

- ✓ Use a journal with a big enough portal

- ✓ Consider moving on to the SOAP structure

- ✓ Dare to write down the promptings of Holy Spirit, what you think he might be saying to you

- ✓ Allow yourself to get it wrong. You are not necessarily going to tell other people what God has said to you; e.g., "Thus sayeth the Lord…" So, write freely

- ✓ Take joy in this aspect of your discipleship

- ✓ See where he takes you with this.

CHAPTER 6
The Perfect Lie

"What I journal feels like rubbish..."

I went through a period, fairly early on, when I approached journalling as something I had to write perfectly. It seemed to become so sacred, it scared me. (Interesting how *scared* is a scrambled anagram of the word *sacred*.) I would pause, then freeze, in front of the blank page.

I have nothing today, I would think, *at least nothing worthy of my journal.*

This is one of the major and most persistent inhibitors to our free expression on the page: we seek perfection. This troubling thought comes from that voice that I call our **Inner Critic**. The Inner Critic says something like, *You can't write! What you will write will be awful!* We all have an Inner Critic. Some call it the **Judge**. Author Steven Pressfield calls it **Resistance**.[17]

Perfectionism is a hungry beast that is never satisfied. You can look at your writing and be disappointed. Most times, perfectionism feeds on comparison. You can compare what you have written to the written eloquence of others. Don't do this; it is not smart! Paul wrote this about the folly of comparing ourselves and our work with others around us:

> We do not dare to classify or compare ourselves with some who commend themselves. When they measure themselves by themselves and compare themselves with themselves, they are not wise.
> **2 Corinthians 10:12 (NIV)**

We have all heard that Inner Critic. It is powerful. So what can we do in response to it?

Morning Pages

One practice of detoxing ourselves from perfectionism is something I came across in Julia Cameron's brilliant book, *The Artist's Way*.[18] She advocates doing something she calls **Morning Pages**. In her writing workshops, she asks her students to write three handwritten pages of stream-of-consciousness thoughts each day. This routine is an excellent practice for those who want to write for others or to unlock their creativity in any form, but I believe the soul journal can be a vehicle for that as well.

Consider this: as we journal our soul thoughts in private, before God, we do much of this detoxing. We expose the Inner Critic and can assess most positively whether there is truth there. Moreover, the Holy Spirit will help us. He does, after all, lead us into all truth.

What the professional creatives do

A painting is never finished. It just stops in interesting places.
Pablo Picasso

It seems that artists, writers, choreographers, comedians, song writers and composers have developed certain approaches to their work, that circumvent this barrier. It is worth noting that such people are not immune to the perfect lie.

Although journalling is private, we can still learn from these creatives who create for others. In fact, I've come to believe that we *all* have to do this to live at our best. It matters not whether we write for a living or whether we are pursuing soul journalling for our own private conversation with God, these approaches have value in getting past the perfectionist lie.

So, what do they do? What most professional creatives *don't* do is to expect quality results immediately. What they often start to do is quite surprising; they start by getting rough ideas committed to their medium.

For example, the difference between professional writers and the rest of us is merely this: they will not allow perfectionism to deter their writing. They get on and commit their words to the page, nevertheless. These writers are clear in their own mind that what they are aiming for is not perfection. They simply get their flow of thoughts down on paper. This practice will be cathartic in itself.

Professional creatives do three things in an order most of us don't:

- They **start**. They sketch. They practice. They draft. They get anything down to play with an idea. They get that lump of clay out onto the turntable.

- They aim for **quantity**, not quality. They go for volume of expression around an idea or a problem. The composer, Robert Fritz, says that most people picture an artist, for example, as agonising for days up in their lonely studio, waiting for the Muse to come and inspire them. Not so, says Fritz. They busy themselves with work-a-day disciplines to create volume. Most authors, from Stephen King to Jeffrey Archer, set themselves daily writing targets — so many words, so many pages, or so many bars, etc.

- Then they **hone** and **refine**.

When I do this, I find that it often silences that critical voice. As I write, I surprise myself with my insights. So, I say to myself, *I'm just going to put all my thoughts down, stupid ones as well as profound ones. I'll sift them later…maybe.*

That 'maybe' is important; it can remove any perfectionist inhibition from my attempts to write. This is why techniques like Morning Pages work.

Now, when I journal, I can journal my best or be inhibited by the beast of perfectionism. Best or beast? That is my choice. And choice is freedom.

All this may seem counter-intuitive to you at first. Just writing anything down looks the wrong way to go. Consider then this analogy: the writer's initial rough drafts are like that lump of potter's clay. The more they draft, the more they have to work with in terms of feelings, ideas, and arguments. The lump of clay is not the end goal, but the means to an end. The potter then fashions this into something perhaps beautiful and exquisite. So does the writer. So does God as you co-create your soul journal together.

> … there is that charming story of Hokusai, the great Japanese painter and maker of woodcuts around 1800. Once somebody asked him for a painting of a rooster. He said, "OK, come back in a week." When the man came, he asked for postponement; two weeks more. Then again, two months, then half a year. Then after three years the man was so angry, that he refused to

wait any longer. Hokusai said that he would have it there and then. He took his brush and his paper and drew a beautiful rooster in a short time. Then the man was really furious. 'Why do you keep me waiting for years if you can do it in such as short time?' 'You don't understand,' said Hokusai, 'come with me.' And he took the man to his studio, and showed him that all the walls were covered with drawings of roosters he had been doing over the last three years. Out of that came mastery.

Hans R. Rookmaker
Art Needs No Justification, pp.61-62.

We can learn from the professional creatives, if we are prepared just to show up and journal, even if we feel empty. Sometimes, as with my experience that I referred to earlier at Schipol airport, the results can surprise us later.

Your Inner Critic *May* have Value

Is our Inner Critic really the devil, the enemy of our souls? Not always. I suspect that Christians tend to give the evil one too much credit. However, I also believe that satan will use our critical faculties for his own purposes, but critical thinking was not his invention.

The Inner Critic is often useful, as long as we listen to it in the right moments.

When your creative self needs to take over, tell the Inner Critic to go away; tell it that you will need it to show up later, but not now. You may even need to vocalise this, saying it out loud. (I'm serious.) The brain cannot distinguish what you speak from what you truly believe. Also, your words have more authority over your mind that you perhaps realise.

Allow me to repeat: in soul journalling, your audience is exclusively you and God. So, the editing role of the Inner Critic is *hardly ever needed*. However, if your journalling is shared with others, then your Inner Critic can become valuable. If I turn something Holy Spirit and I have been working through together, and then I feel it is valuable to share with a wider audience, yes, I will allow the Inner Critic in me to edit it for that audience.

A Test of the Inner Critic

Like any of our inner narratives, we need to see how they measure up with the character of our God, and bring to bear the invaluable counsel of Holy Spirit, who is available to us all.

> There is therefore now no condemnation
> for those who are in Christ Jesus.
> **Romans 8:1**

This is pivotal verse in Paul's letter to the Romans. God may correct his beloved children. Does he ever condemn us? Never! Romans 8:1 makes that very clear.

So, who does condemn us and our work? The accuser of the brethren. (Revelation 12:10)

Materialists do not recognise that we have an spiritual enemy that seeks to tempt and seduce us to being less than powerful. I am not saying that what Stephen King, Jeffrey Archer, Steven Pressfield and others describe as Resistance, the Inner Critic, and so on, is *always* the enemy of our souls. No, not at all. We have a critical, evaluative faculty in all of us that is God-given and useful. However, we need to guard against the Inner Critic, albeit useful at times, when it begins to attack not just what we created, but our very identity. Our self-analysis is then doing the work of our enemy. That is never helpful and needs to be rebuked.

Circling Back

When the Spirit of truth comes, he will guide you into all the truth,
for he will not speak on his own authority, but whatever he hears he
will speak, and he will declare to you the things that are to come.
John 16:13

Looking back, I realise that I have been far too focused on immediate results
instead of the *process*, when it comes to the ways of the Spirit, who leads me.
Perfectionism can beat me up because the outcome on the page is not as perfect
or as original as my soul journal was yesterday.

I notice that I am led back to the same themes again and again; and this
is despite working through some books of the Bible systematically. In fact, in
conversation, often friends and family will mention something that I had only
been journalling that very morning.

When this happens to us, what's going on?

It is Holy Spirit leading us in his curriculum. He is not concerned with our
desired outcomes in the same way as we might, but he knows when we need to
meditate on something again, maybe deeper this time. It's not primarily about
cognitive information; instead, this is our soul transformation in action. It's a
great mystery. When we decide that we need to own our soul transformation, he
leads us. Like many aspects of the kingdom, when we take ownership in faith,
he acts.

So, perfectionism might be my way of trying to complete something.
Meditation on old truths is Holy Spirit's way of returning my heart to a subject I
previously understood only superficially, with my reason.

For example, at the time of writing, I keep being led back to Proverbs 4:23.
At the moment, I am meditating on the English Standard Version of this:

Keep your heart with all vigilance,
for from it flow the springs of life.

When I realise that Holy Spirit is returning me to some truth, and I trust him with that journey; as I meditate on that text, he leads me into new depths of understanding and application to my life. This deeper knowledge and experience seem to emerge and flow as I trust him and meditate again on old truths.

Could this be, then, that Holy Spirit is leading us to hone and refine steps in a manner we considered earlier in this chapter among the professional creatives? He leads us in his paths of righteousness; and sometimes those paths appear circular.

However, the main point I want to stress here is that we are journalling for ourselves and God. When we soul journal, we do it for ourselves; it's not for others. We get it down, however imperfect that may seem to our Inner Critic.

Activation: Perfectionism is Irrelevant

So respond to this tyrant of perfectionism is by declaring out loud:

I am kind to myself. I do not need to write perfectly.

I write for my Lord and me. He and I are the audience.

Then, if you need to, rebuke the accuser. Tell him to go; as, your journal is off-limits to him; he has no place during your soul journal time.

Finally, ask yourself and Holy Spirit these questions:

- Are there any themes emerging in my journal, those areas of soul transformation that come back to me again and again?

- Are you, Lord, inviting me to go deeper in this area?

CHAPTER 7

Abundance

*What I work out in private
is bound to express itself in public.*

The good person out of the good treasure of his heart produces
good, and the evil person out of his evil treasure produces evil,
for out of the abundance of the heart his mouth speaks.

Luke 6:45

In a later chapter on *Blessings*,[19] I explore the dynamic of Holy Spirit spilling out into other areas of our lives as we soul journal. Whatever we are full of begins to express itself in multiple ways. The concept behind the slang insult, *"You're full of it!"* does have some truth to it. Here, I want to explore some expressions of journalling that spill out into other parts of our lives, and how I track this from my journal to the practice of my daily work.

As I have stressed, the journal is a private matter. But what I work out in private is bound to express itself in public. So, what I discover and meditate upon in my journal has relevance, for example, in how I do my work.

As I explain in my earlier book, *Leading Yourself,* I also keep a daybook for organising my thoughts around my work, identifying my priority for that day, and taking notes such as when I manage a team. I have a method where my daily planning takes the form of keeping a **Gratitude List** on one page and my **Daily Heads-Up** on the opposite page.

It looks like this:

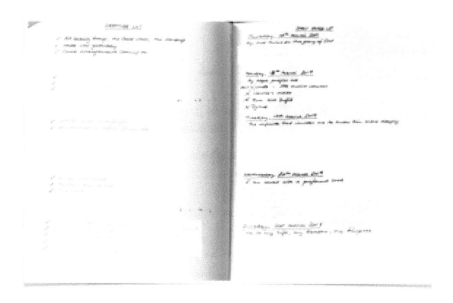

An example of my daybook pages with parts blurred

I use an A5 dot-grid notebook. In this example, where most of my entries have been blurred, on the left-facing page, each day I list those things for which I am thankful. I aim for 3-5 things to give express thanks; this is my **Gratitude List**. Often, these items are from what I experienced the previous day.

On the right-facing page, is my **Daily Heads-Up**, where I do my day planning. However, I write a declaration about who I am or whom my Lord is to me, based upon what I had been journalling or what he has said to me.

In this way, I intentionally bridge what I have been discovering, or have been reminded of, in my journal into how I attempt to shape my day ahead.

Let's take a closer look at gratitude and declarations.

Gratitude

> Give thanks to the God of heaven, for his
> steadfast love endures forever.
> **Psalm 136:26**

I could have chosen any one of many verses about giving thanks in Scripture since thanksgiving is such a significant theme. This significance, in itself, is very revealing. God places great value in his children being thankful. It seems that in the act of giving thanks, we find value. We are created to live at our optimum from a place of thankfulness.

As I disciplined myself to express thanks to God, I found my heart shifting. Because of our fight or flight defences, we all have a leaning towards noticing the negative, the *negativity bias*.[20] The news media exploits this to get our attention. After a while, all we can see is what is terrible in the world. Our mood becomes negative, and we invite persistent fear and depression into our souls.

There is no fear in the Kingdom. When I begin to give thanks, I reconnect with an essential reality of the Kingdom. Thanking God for the good things that I experience is generative. Thanksgiving, or the diligent daily expression of it, reconnects me with the atmosphere of heaven. I became more open to joy, laughter and possibilities. Thanksgiving helps me live from heaven.

Declarations

A declaration is a positive statement about who I am, who I am destined to become, or who God is for me in this particular moment. The declarations for the days in the particular week of my daybook shown above are:

My life turns on the glory of God

The Infinite God invites me to know him more deeply

I am loved with a profound love

He is my Life, my Reason, my Purpose

My hope purifies me

These are summaries of something in each day's journal.

Activation

Try this companion journalling for yourself.

In your Daybook, reflect on:

- What three people or things am I grateful for right now?

- What is the Lord saying is my priority, my one thing, for today?

And throughout the day, after significant moments, meetings, or pauses, journal:

- What just happened?

- What feelings did it provoke in me?

- What is the Spirit saying to me?

- What can I learn from this?

CHAPTER 8
Media

The media with which we journal matters

There is a decision about the medium with which we are going to journal: should we take the digital route or the handwriting route? Marshall McLuhan, a Canadian philosopher in the last century, famously said

The medium is the message

When it comes to soul journalling, though, that is not true. The message is the conversation, irrespective of the medium. However, choosing between digital soul journalling or handwritten media might be more to do with the *process* with which each medium helps us.

McLuhan's fellow countryman, journalist Clive Thompson, recently went on record, at a presentation on YouTube, that handwriting works well for working through ideas, for reflective writing.[21] Whereas typing has the edge on getting your ideas down before they escape your mind.

Some of my friends journal before the Lord on their computers, and do it well. But I feel there is a lot more going for the medium of a pen on paper.

I admit that I am biased — everyone is — and one of my conscious biases is towards handwriting as the best medium for soul journalling. While this book is about soul journalling in general, it would be remiss of me not to expand on the virtues of handwriting, in particular.

My advice is to **begin with a handwritten journal**. There are, as we shall see, many benefits to handwriting.

Even so, these days there is a case to be made for a hybrid approach: both handwriting *and* digital.

Awkward with Handwriting

Handwriting might be a challenge for you, particularly since we are now so used to typing. You might find it awkward, as many are just not used to it. If this is the case, then you do not need the added challenge of developing your handwriting muscles and learning to write legibly. Instead, I recommend you use some app on your computer, tablet or even your phone.

As I went on in soul journalling, I used whatever was to hand. I even had seasons when I switched to digital journalling

In the digital world, it is better if you can create a distraction-free electronic environment, or at least minimise those distractions. Also, in the digital world, the size of the digital portal, the screen size, also can matter, as we considered in an earlier chapter.

Furthermore, with digital journalling, there is often a choice about the device we use. For some years now, I have had *four* such devices to choose from: my desktop, laptop, tablet and smartphone. And not all these devices are equal, otherwise I couldn't justify having four! Each as positives and negatives to do with journalling. Now, if my choice at any particular time is between my tablet or my smartphone, I'd prefer the tablet, because it offers me a bigger portal than does my phone.

For the most part, though, I revert back to pen and paper.

Rediscovering Analog

In recent years, there has been a return to so-called *analog* media; that is, traditional pen and paper. This rediscovery is not a wholesale abandonment of technology, but rather a rebalancing of work between the two media. After many of us had attempted to pursue the paperless office, we rediscovered the delight and power of pen and paper.

For example, many have reacted against the growing number of productivity apps by adopting written notebook-based methods. Perhaps one of the most popular of these methods is the **Bullet Journal**, a productivity system based on structured pages in a hand-written notebook.[22]

An Example of a Bullet Journal [Photo by Estée Janssens on Unsplash]

So who pioneered this system? Was it some old traditionalist? No, it comes from a surprising source: a young digital native, a New York graphics designer, Ryder Carroll, whose trade requires high-order skills with sophisticated software programs such as Photoshop and Illustrator. These applications require long and intense focus on a computer screen to get quality results.

Carroll discovered a benefit from breaking away, for short periods, from his habitual work environment of the screen, for him to order his life on paper, in what he came to call the Bullet Journal.

So, have we got it wrong with technology? Is paper now better than electronic media? The answer seems to be that, for many of us, *both* have their merits, particularly in combination. This isn't a question of *either* computer technology *or* pen and paper, but rather a productive complementary partnership of both.

However, when I approach my journal as a means to reflect and meditate, breaking away from technology helps me achieve achieve exactly that..

Bi-Modal Journalling

One concern you may have about handwritten journals could be that they cannot be stored in a way that allows them to be referenced later.

Well, first, may I remind you that the content of the journal is not our primary goal in soul journalling. It is the process, the in-the-moment processing with God on the page that matters. So, being able to reference later is a secondary function of the media you use to journal.

However, there is a solution to this. We do not need to transcribe what we have handwritten by typing the journal entry all over again. I use an app called **Evernote** which can access the camera on my phone and scan and store a written page.[1] It is as simple as taking a photo of a page. Once captured, the page is sent to your password-protected account in the cloud. You can then add further tags to identify a particular entry that is significant for you.

Evernote has done a great job on this. Other applications like it, such as Notion, are still catching up with the simplicity of doing this.

I go a step further with this. Do you remember my discussion on the SOAP journalling approach in chapter 5, *Growing*? Well, I went on later to describe how I developed the title for each journal as a positive declaration.

> For example, as I write this, today's journal title is this declaration: *God is doing amazing things through us.* This relates to reflections on what happened yesterday at a meeting I led, and to some friends' journey in the Netherlands who have a wonderful dream that is becoming a reality.

---

1   See more detail on this in the Appendix on Digital Journalling.

When I complete a journal entry for the day, I capture it into Evernote with my smartphone's camera, into a particular notebook reserved for this called 'My journal entries.' It is at this point I give the entry a title. What Evernote does is that it then store my entries in sequence with the titles listed in date order, thus:

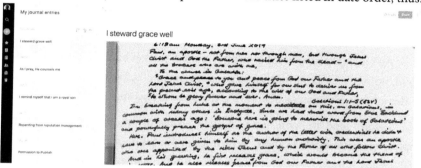

Screenshot of my Evernote notebook called 'My journal entries',
showing an entry titled with a declaration "I steward grace well",
with other recent titles listed on the left

So, by default Evernote can create your index of your journal and it provides you with a growing history of your entries.

Portable Stationery

Thoughts can strike us at the most inconvenient times. Often these are insights that we need to write down for soulful meditations. The brain does not necessarily deliver these insights to our consciousness at the moments that we think are appropriate, such as when we are at a desk during a block of time that we devote to journalling. Thoughts come at apparently random, sometimes inconvenient moments: in the shower, during a conversation, during sung worship in a church, and so on.

Regarding worship, it seems that, when we are open to the ultimate Reality, all kinds of ideas and thoughts come to the surface of our awareness.

As I have mentioned, one of my main forms of exercise is walking. I like to walk in the countryside. And, of course, as the oxygen begins to pump through my brain, I get some rich ideas and thoughts about my current writing project. So I capture these with an audio recording app on my smartphone. It is simple, easy, and the transcription process afterwards often gives me further insights. Usually, a walk can become a very fertile activity during a writing project.

As I mentioned above, I also carry a small pocket book and pencil. This is good, not only for keeping a to-do list with me and actively maintained, but it is also a reassuring means of knowing that if an idea comes to me I can trap it.

I don't tend to write notes directly using my mobile phone. For me, capturing my thoughts as audio recordings or photos on a phone is much easier than typing a note. And, as we considered under chapter 2 on *Noise*, a mobile phone can also be prone to distraction. There are a lot of other messages and apps clamouring for my attention. Also, a mobile phone may be perhaps more unsociable in certain contexts. For example, if I'm talking with someone, I think it is less discourteous in most circles I move in for me to ask for a moment to jot something into my pocket book than to whip out my smartphone. Also, it can honour the conversation as something rich and important for me, by this handwritten signal.

So, consider this: what if we were to journal at these times as well? What if communion with God through our soul could continue through the day in short sentences and paragraphs?

Activation

Sometimes we only learn our preferences by playing. As we try new things, we discover what suits us.

- If your preference so far has been to journal on a digital platform, by phone, tablet, laptop or desktop, then try paper journalling for ten days. Reflect on how you found the process once you become at ease with writing or drawing out your journal on paper.

- If, on the other hand, you have only ever journalled on paper, try the opposite: for ten days journal on your favourite app.

- After ten days, make your own assessment of what suits you.

~~~~~~

PART 3 - MAKING SENSE OF ALL THIS

In Part 3, I want to share with you some of the patterns I have noticed in soul journalling, as well as the understanding I have grown in along the way. We can all make better sense of what is happening in us and around us when we develop the soul journalling habit and start talking with God on the page. This is not so much about my personal journey of discovery and discipleship, nor about what might be immediately practical to you, but is more what I believe God is doing in all of us when we practice soul journalling.

CHAPTER 9

Blessings

More than you can ever ask or imagine

I have already touched on quite a few of the benefits we discover as we soul journal. These include, in no particular order:

✓ Getting **clarity** as we write our thoughts and feelings down

✓ Resolving and reducing the **noise** in our soul

✓ **Slowing ourselves down** and entering more into **deep thinking**

✓ Greater **focus**

✓ Growing in **self-awareness**

✓ Experiencing moments of **freedom from drivenness**

✓ A means of releasing ourselves into greater **creativity**

✓ An ability to **pray** more intentionally

✓ A route to **healing emotional pain**

✓ **Hearing God** more clearly

✓ A place to **value and nurture** what God is saying to us, and what he is doing in and through us

✓ The working space for **soul transformation**, our work-in-progress renewal

✓ A medium of having powerful **conversations with God**

✓ An increasing experience of **joy**

✓ Capturing significant **insights** that may be useful to others

Let us explore some of these more deeply.

Overflowing into many blessings

> Whoever believes in me, as the Scripture has said,
> 'Out of his heart will flow rivers of living water.'
> **John 7:38**

Charles Duhigg talks about *keystone habits*, that is, those habits that have multiple other benefits supporting other habits.[23] In Duhigg's terms, the practice of keeping a soul journal is a keystone habit. Again and again, people tell me that their journalling is an enriching discipline, a discipline that spills over into other areas of their lives.

Wherever Holy Spirit is at work, he is no respecter of boundaries; that is to say, his blessings spill out into other areas of our lives as well. His rivers of living water splash everywhere. This heavenly dynamic is no less evident than when it comes to consistent journalling with him.

Insight

> Let the word of Christ dwell in you richly, teaching and admonishing
> one another in all wisdom, singing psalms and hymns and
> spiritual songs, with thankfulness in your hearts to God.
> **Colossians 3:16**

Then there is something less obvious about this spilling over into life outside journal time. The combination of focus, particularly on his Word, gaining clarity about our soul, listening to the living God, giving thanks to him, and declaring truths about ourselves and him; it all combines to insight, discernment and wisdom.

> Now when they saw the boldness of Peter and John, and
> perceived that they were uneducated, common men, they were
> astonished. And they recognised that they had been with Jesus.
> **Acts 4:13**

Again and again, I have found the very way I phrase words in conversations with friends and clients begins to impact them, in ways that surprise me. We could say that we mobilise a sort of wisdom that is anointed by Holy Spirit. It is wisdom from above, yes; but that only explains part of why it happens. As disciples, diligent in our conversations with God, we begin to access the mind of Christ within us. As the soul is renewed, we lay bare that mind of Christ that had always been there in our spirit. We begin to think and talk more like Jesus would think and talk.

> "For who has understood the mind of the Lord so as to instruct him?" But we have the mind of Christ.
> **1 Corinthians 2:16**

Sure, the major theme of this book is that soul journalling is extraordinarily powerful. However, its power can be limited if we categorise it and isolate it from the rest of our lives. We can choose to create a sort of religious silo of journal time, and build a case that it is spiritual and that the rest of our day is different. I don't believe Holy Spirit is contained that easily. Nor should we attempt to constrain what he does in such a restrictive wineskin.

> Beloved, we are God's children now, and what we will be has not yet appeared; but we know that when he appears we shall be like him, because we shall see him as he is.
> **1 John 3:2**

The religious spirit attempts to confine a disciple's faith to the synagogue, the church, the chapel or the secret place of prayer. But our God is wild and loose; and as we see him, we become like him.

> We need to move from a visitation culture to a habitation culture.
> **Graham Cooke**

In the previous chapter on *Abundance*, we began to come against this religious silo mentality by bridging our soul journalling into a daybook, for example. Our calling, as disciples filled with Holy Spirit, is to experience the presence of God all the time, and not lapse into a visitation culture, where God only breaks through to us on exceptional occasions.

Activation

Next time you journal

- Review your previous day's entry and ask yourself the question:

  What could I have done to live out of that conversation more?

Do not take on shame or guilt about this; we do not do that this side of the Cross. Christ has dealt with all our shame and guilt once and for all.

- Instead, consider as you finish your journal today, ask yourself:

  How can I better express this conversation, this revelation in the day ahead?

Heightened Focus

"Therefore do not be anxious, saying, 'What shall we eat?' or 'What shall we drink?' or 'What shall we wear?' For the Gentiles seek after all these things, and your heavenly Father knows that you need them all. But seek first the kingdom of God and his righteousness, and all these things will be added to you."

Matthew 6:31-33

There is something about writing out coherent sentences that draws us into a state of more in-depth focus. It is immersive. Furthermore, in developing the habit of keeping a soul journal, we find that it helps us develop several other strengths that build a pattern into our work.

I can shape my working week in blocks of deep, concentrated focus, something I had not achieved before I kept my soul journal. Such blocks have helped me author books and build online resources, as well as improve my service to my clients.

Also soul journalling helps us to focus upon matters more intentionally, at will. Our ability to focus is as much about being aware of our life priorities as it is about being able to stay attentive to one task for longer. Soul journalling invites the disciple to seek first the kingdom of God and its righteousness. That is the disciple's priority.

If distraction makes us run after far too many agendas, focus helps us attend to that which is the most important. The kingdom is ultimately recognised by the disciple as Holy Spirit's agenda at that moment for them. What is he saying to us **right now**? If we seek the kingdom, we must seek the King.

Greater Clarity

The unexamined life is not worth living.
Socrates

Michael Hyatt talks about taking the role of the journalist.[24] This kind of journalism introduces a significant benefit; it helps us make a more objective assessment of our experiences. We get emotions out of our soul and onto paper. It is as if we are standing outside of the action and observing ourselves, our thoughts and emotions. Then we can assess our thoughts and reactions rather more objectively.

Thus, our soul journal becomes a powerful way of building a private feedback loop into our life. We learn to review and adjust our behaviours accordingly.

To take time to think is to gain time to live.
Nancy Kline[25]

Often, ignoring those swirling thoughts in our head seems to make them whirl around even more. As soon as we commit them to paper, the storm begins to calm.

We all attempt to make sense of our world, at least to some degree, and we often come to very different conclusions about it. Journalling slows us down to observe ourselves and the world more carefully. Two realms open up for us: the external world of events and experiences, and the internal world of rational thinking, of our values, beliefs, emotions, and maybe even the lies and distortions that we have lived with for too long.

Our soul journal invites us to reflect on our life, often by looking at the previous day, in such a way that it helps us make better sense of things.

Without this clarity, we can become anxious or overwhelmed in our confusion, more prone to get stuck in thought patterns that produce the same sub-optimal actions again and again.

The soul journal helps us process our confusion. And usually, it helps us to break out of that confusion into greater clarity.

Creativity

> In the journal I do not just express myself more openly
> than I could to any person; I create myself.
>
> **Susan Sontag**

Journalling is a creative exercise. When we begin, there's a blank page. When we have finished, there is substance. For the disciple, creativity is an expression of being made in the image of the Creator.

As we considered in the chapter on *The Perfect Lie*, all professional creatives come to realise that their first attempts, their first draft, their first sketch, their first step, is usually far from adequate in some way. They learn to live with that and not let it deter them. They learn to push through this imperfection. They develop mechanisms for allowing the Inner Critic within them to come back later to review the alleged rubbish they have created. In the same way, we learn to switch off that Inner Critic which we all have, long enough for creativity to flow.

Creativity requires us to reframe what we do, to approach it differently. Transformation, the re-creating of our soul, happens when we journal with God, and this is co-creating with God, as much as the external co-creating of a gardener or farmer with God.

Summary: Blessings in Keeping a Soul Journal

Soul journalling

✓ Is a *keystone habit* common in many outstanding achievers, spinning off other powerful life habits

✓ Can improve our prayer

✓ Develops our ability to *focus for longer and focus more deeply*. It opens the way for us to do in-depth work outside of soul journalling

✓ Heightens our focus on the most important: the kingdom of God and its righteousness

✓ Becomes a vehicle for us to make sense of our internal and external world, breaking out from confusion to *greater clarity*

✓ Is *creative*, an activity where we express the image of the Creator within us

Activation:

- Use the points in this chapter's summary as affirmations you declare over yourself. For example:

In my journalling I grow in prayer.

In my soul journal, I co-create with God.

I am growing in clarity about my life and the world around me.

I can focus for concentrated periods on the one thing the King wants me to attend to.

As I soul journal with my Lord, rivers of living water flow out of me.

- Say these declarations over yourself before you start your regular daily session of soul journalling, and see what happens...

CHAPTER 10
Soul

"I like your Earth Suit."

I have called this kind of journalling *soul journalling* deliberately. But what do we mean when we talk about our **soul**? There is a lot of confusion around this term, as often happens when spiritual language is adopted into popular culture.

What I want to do here is to set out the distinctions between spirit, soul and body, and suggest why these distinctions matter. I discovered the importance of this distinction in the last ten years and when I did, it made a massive difference to me.

What makes you tick?

I used to work for an organisation where one of the directors, a fierce and aggressive man, had a reputation for asking people he had just met, "What makes you tick?" He never needed to ask me, but my response might have been, "That's for you to find out!"

However, the fact remains that the question, if asked by ourselves of ourselves, is an excellent one: what makes me tick?

The Bible is clear on this matter. At its simplest, we are all made up of a spirit, a soul, and a body.

> Now may the God of peace himself sanctify you completely,
> and may your whole spirit and soul and body be kept
> blameless at the coming of our Lord Jesus Christ.
> **1 Thessalonians 5:23**

Our body and our soul are mortal; they will die.

> Behold, all souls are mine; the soul of the father as well as
> the soul of the son is mine: the soul who sins shall die.
> **Ezekiel 18:4**

> And just as it is appointed for man to die once, and after that
> comes judgment, so Christ, having been offered once to bear
> the sins of many, will appear a second time, not to deal with
> sin but to save those who are eagerly waiting for him.
> **Hebrews 9:27-28**

The body and, to some degree, the soul (also known as the *mind*), can be observed and measured, and so are acknowledged by science and thus are of interest to research.

This is not the case with our spirit. Perhaps because our spirit is not observable by our five senses, the distinction between soul (mind) and spirit is something we need some help with:

> For the word of God is living and active, sharper than any two-edged
> sword, ***piercing the division of soul and spirit***, of joints and
> marrow and discerning the thoughts and intentions of the heart.
> **Hebrews 4:12 [Emphasis mine]**

So, it seems that there is a distinction between our spirit and our soul. The spirit of a person is that part of us made in the image of God. Our spirit is immortal. It is not usually observable by material means.

> God is spirit; and those who worship him
> must worship in spirit and truth.
> **John 4:24**

This text is where Jesus explained to the Samaritan woman that our spirit is vital to our being able to worship God. So, if each of us is made up of a spirit, a soul and a body, how might we visualise that?

Here is a diagram that may help, although it is limited:

Here we see our spirit, soul and body as three overlapping entities. Each overlaps the other because, to some extent, they can influence and affect each other. For example, there is some considerable two-way traffic between the soul and the body. The soul, which sometimes is called the **mind**, the way we think and feel, can make us physically well or sick; we can worry ourselves to death. And the flow can work the other way too: pain can also impair our ability to think clearly and we can allow physical pain to drag us down emotionally.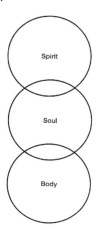

> Therefore, if anyone is in Christ, he is a new creation. The
> old has passed away; behold, the new has come.
> **2 Corinthians 5:17**

When Paul described the early Christ-followers in Corinth as a new creation, he was not referring to their bodies, nor even their souls, but the spirit that was within every human being.

A radical transformation happens when we believe and follow Jesus. We have been born again into the new life of the Kingdom. Our spirit is perfect, a new creation, in which the Holy Spirit, himself inhabits.

> In him you also, when you heard the word of truth,
> the gospel of your salvation, and believed in him,
> were sealed with the promised Holy Spirit.
> **Ephesians 1:13**

We are a new creation. Holy Spirit takes up residence within us. Not only that, but he has sealed our spirit, such that our spirit is now perfect.

However, we have a command as disciples to be transformed by the renewing of our minds (Romans 12:2). Our spirit has already been transformed, so what is Paul meaning here, in writing to the Roman believers? This does not relate to our spirit but rather to our soul — the habitual ways we think, feel and react. So, the relationship between our spirit and our soul is more of a one-way flow, from our spirit to our soul; our spirit can affect our soul, but not the other way around. And this is good news. It means that I am forever a new creation. It is my soul that needs renewal. That is how I can be a new creation *and* in need of transformation.

Ghosts or Giants?

> But we have this treasure in jars of clay, to show that the
> surpassing power belongs to God and not to us.
> **2 Corinthians 4:7**

The popular understanding of what a *spirit* could be is that it is something ghostly, ethereal and small. And we tend to project that onto our reading of the Bible.

But what if it was the other way around? What if our spirit is the most significant, the most vital, the most enduring, the most essential, and the most substantial part of us? What if our spirit is **more** substantial than our body?

> I saw my mother the day before she died. Then I saw her body
> the next morning after she had passed away; we had arrived at
> the hospital too late. When I saw her corpse, though, I knew
> she was not there. Her spirit had gone. All that was left was
> the body that had failed her.

This was a further important realisation for me as I came to grips with my own transformation.

> On the evening of that day, the first day of the week, the doors
> being locked where the disciples were for fear of the Jews, Jesus
> came and stood among them and said to them, "Peace be with
> you." When he has said this, he showed them his hands and his
> side. Then the disciples were glad when they saw the Lord.
> **John 20:19-20**

When Jesus rose from the dead, his body could do things that no normal body could do. He walked through walls into locked rooms, able to appear and disappear. Theologians say that he now has a spiritual body. It is a body where Jesus is recognisable, but it is a body that is much more integrated with his Spirit. His disciples could still touch him, and he could eat food with them.

So, what if Jesus could, after his resurrection, appear to his disciples in a locked room because the walls were **less** substantial than his risen, spiritual body?[26] Maybe this material, temporary world is **less** substantial than the spirit world. That Spirit world is known as by the term 'heaven.'

Now, this is a concept does not quite fit the popular concept of a spirit as a phantasm or some sort of ethereal ghost, does it?

I Like Your Earth Suit

When we realise that we are an immortal spirit with a temporary earth suit, everything changes. Our view of ourselves changes. Our view of our mortal soul changes.

As I mentioned above, picturing this in two dimensions has its limitations, but consider this second diagram:

Here is a further thought: what if, instead of thinking of ourselves as a *body* with a soul and a spirit, we might better think of ourselves as a **spirit** with a body and a soul? As we cooperate with Holy Spirit, our spirit renews our mind, that is, our soul. Our soul comes into alignment with the reality of our spirit.

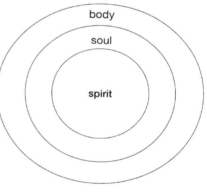

And there remains the potential two-way dynamic between the soul and the body. Health in our soul brings health to our body.

The Real Frontier of Renewal

> Do not be conformed to this world, but be transformed by the
> renewal of your mind, that by testing you may discern what is
> the will of God, what is good and acceptable and perfect.
> **Romans 12:2**

When we use the word *renewal* in the church, we often confine it to corporate manifestations and expressions of worship. It is clear from this text that Paul saw renewal as something far more profound and extensive than that.

If we are a new creation, then why do we need transformation? Clearly, we all still do need some home improvement. We are not yet as we should be. I may be a new creation, but this earth suit I'm wearing is creaking a bit!

This is where having a tripartite understanding of our nature — as spirit, soul and body — begins to make sense. Our spirit may now be a new creation, yet our body is fading away. The soul, for most of us, still has some way to go to catch up with the glorious spirit that is within us. When I confused my soul with my spirit, I was also confused about whether I really am a new creation, when I have sinned. Now, I consider my spirit as new. Yes, we can still sin, but it does not change who we essentially are.

> We don't have a sin nature, we have a sin habit.
> **Graham Cooke**

We are saints who sin, rather than sinners who repent. This way of viewing ourselves and how we grow in Christlikeness is profoundly different from the religious mindset most of us grew up with.

It is our mortal soul, which we refer to as our *mind*, which includes our emotions and our will, that is still a work-in-progress.

> So we do not lose heart. Though our outer self is wasting
> away, our inner self is being renewed day by day. For this light
> momentary affliction is preparing for us an eternal weight of
> glory beyond all comparison, as we look not to the things that
> are seen but to the things that are unseen. For the things that are
> seen are transient, but the things that are unseen are eternal.
> **2 Corinthian 4: 16-18**

Now, I'm not claiming that our body is unimportant or since it is temporary, that it doesn't matter. On the contrary, I believe this is part of our stewardship for each of us to take good care of our body. We need to exercise appropriately, and eat sensibly. Our body is the vehicle, for the moment, in the way we serve people and it is what people see as us, so our body is an expression of the glory of God in us. We are going places; we need our physical vehicle, our body, in the best condition possible.

But, when it comes to the soul, why can't God just do this soul transformation for us? He has saved us and made us a new creation; why can't he finish the job off?

It seems that God invites each of us to be a willing participant in our own soul transformation. He values our free will, our ability to freely choose, too much to do a total makeover on us. He wants us to partner with him in this renewal. So, we choose daily to follow as a disciple, and we choose to grow; or not. Faith invites our choices. God seems to put a high premium on our expressing faith in him.

And without faith it is impossible to please him…
Hebrews 11:6

And in all this choosing, God intends it to be a relational process, rather than a merely academically theological one, or even merely some kind of moral workout.

So, what's Journalling Got to Do with It?

You might be thinking,

What's all this soul and spirit stuff got to do with journalling?

Quite a lot, I believe. Being transformed is about our taking responsibility for our transformation by the renewal of our mind, renewal by growing in relationship with God. We need some means of diagnosing our soul and working on it with God. Our soul journal can become an important medium in our cooperation with his transformation of us in us.

As soon as we began to consider ourselves as spirit first, with a soul and a body, we come to understand that some parts of us transcend what we recognise as the intellect and the emotions. The spirit part of us is the most important and the most enduring. The soul, then, becomes that internal domain of repentance. We must respond to Holy Spirit in transformation, as a disciple, by our spirit with the help of Holy Spirit. Joyce Meyer rightly said that our battlefield is the mind. And our mind is our soul.

Seeing myself in this way, particularly through my journal meditations, I saw where I really needed to work and grow as a disciple without despairing that my occasional failures and sin had ruined me.

I no longer see myself as a sinner who needs to repent anymore. I am a saint who occasionally sinsand it is from that understanding that I journal.

Activation:

- Reflect on this: *What would it look like to take every thought captive and make it obedient to Christ (2 Cor 10:5)?*

- Spend some time reflecting on what it would be like if your spirit nourished your soul and body.

CHAPTER 11

What I Am Not Saying···

> For every error there is an opposite error.
>
> **Bill Johnson**

I am mindful that a book on spirituality is vulnerable to misinterpretation. Unless you read everything here with generosity and in context, I cannot protect you from that; however, it might be helpful if I list some the extreme interpretations of what I have put before you to show you what I am not saying.

What I am *Not* Saying about Journalling

- *Journalling is the only way to clarify your thoughts.*

  No, gaining clarity in your internal thinking can be achieved in any number of ways including, of course, simple prayer. Activities, such as walking or any kind of cardiovascular exercise, are helpful to many; coaching or counselling; in-depth conversations with a close friend, for example.

- *Everyone must soul journal.*

  No, I'm not making this a new rule. There is no mention in any the biographies of Jesus — the gospels — that he journalled; and yet he is the Pioneer and Perfecter of our faith. (Hebrews 12:2) Yet, the NKJV translates 'Pioneer' as 'Author.' However, for us, it is not an obligation; we have the delight of working out much of our discipleship on the page with him. The danger is that soul journalling could easily become an expression of legalistic religion. In fact, I do not think journalling is for everyone. I have noticed that some of the clients I coach have a style, personality and habits of sense-making that find writing cumbersome. Many are oral processors; they make sense of their own thinking by speaking it out in conversation with the Lord or with others. That's good, and I encourage them to continue with that approach.

Yet, of the people with whom I have come into contact, quite a high proportion of them find freedom and delight when they begin to commit their thoughts to paper. The chances are that you are reading this is because you already have some experience of the power of writing down your own thoughts. Perhaps a more important, a more pertinent question would be: what are you going to do?

What I am *Not* Saying About Noise

- *We will always have noise in our minds.*

No, some people have long periods when they do not. They carry themselves with clarity and without distraction. I wonder if becoming more Christ-like means that we experience longer and longer periods of noise-less thinking. A principal strategy for the best kind soul journalling is to reduce the internal noise to nothing.

- *The noise I am talking about is only of concern to people at work in the information economy.*

No, everyone needs to reduce the external and internal sources of noise.

- *The noise in our minds is always from a spiritual source.*

No, some people suffer from negative thinking and self-induced anxiety, but others from extreme forms of psychosis or from being demonised. This is not the book to explore these areas in any detail. It remains the case, though, that we have constructed lifestyles for ourselves that are conducive to a lot of chatter in our thinking, and we expose ourselves to a lot of invitations to fear. There could be demonic strongholds behind these, but I seek to eliminate or reduce these sources of noise as merely unwelcome distractions.

- *Technology, such as smartphones and email, are evil.*

No! It all depends on how we use these tools. A powerful person chooses how to use a tool, and they are not driven or led by it such that it begins to drive them. They are masters of what they use.

What I am *Not* Saying about Hearing

- *God cannot break through the noise in our lives to speak to us.*

No, God can do anything. However, if I value him enough, I will cooperate by being attentive. I will find ways that work for me to withdraw and speak with him. He delights when his children turn to him and listen of their own choice. He wants me to value what he values. He wants me to appreciate hearing him, as any parent does. So, I will seek moments every day to reduce the internal noise in my life. It is as much about reducing the other noises so that I can hear him more clearly.

- *Soul journalling will make you a genius.*

No, but it could help you become more emotionally intelligent. Emotionally intelligent people have a greater chance of being real with themselves, and of being successful in life.

- *We can only hear God better when we are in the slow lane, the moments of System 2 thinking.*

Clearly, both Elijah and Martha were in states where System 1 thinking was creating much anxiety, and God broke through to them. However, thinking like Elijah and Martha are not to be advised as they were both corrected by God.

- *The transformation of the mind (Romans 12:2) is entirely about changing the physical shape of one's brain.*

  No, but I believe brain neuroplasticity is indicative that we are favouring specific thought patterns in our lives, such as frequent meditation on texts in the Bible, declaring praise and making positive statement over ourselves.

- *That which I write down ascribing to what God says to me is on a par with the Bible.*

  No, I can and do mishear God. I can read into what he might be saying to me. But as I learn to be familiar with the Shepherd's voice *from* Scripture, as I learn to ignore other narratives, I do get better at hearing Him. I believe a primary practice of a disciple is to know the Shepherd's voice.

- *Our bodies don't matter as they are temporary.*

  On the contrary, I believe this is part of our stewardship. We need to care for our bodies, to exercise them appropriately, and eat sensibly. Our bodies are the vehicle, for the moment, in the way we serve God and people; and they are what people see as us, so they are an essential expression of the glory of God in us.

CHAPTER 12

Future

> Dear friends, now we are children of God, and what we will be
> has not yet been made known. But we know that when Christ
> appears, we shall be like him, for we shall see him as he is.
>
> **1 John 3:2**

Traditionally, journalling grew out of keeping a diary. It was less about a record of appointments, but as an emergent history of the journalist's own life and reflections. Most of us have done this at one time or another. We can write, using that powerful word *Yesterday* to chronicle our life, one day at a time. But, for me, I became dissatisfied. It seemed to me that my little life was too confining, too small at the time to really grip me to go on with this practice.

However, when we meet with the living God on the page, our focus in time changes. First, he is the great I AM. We learn from this name, that he is to be found in the present. The present moment is where eternity meets time.

But also, he has plans for each of us. We learn, as Graham Cooke says, that this God is much less interested in talking to us about our flaws and failures, as he is about our destiny, our future with him. There is something profoundly future-oriented in the great I AM. Cooke maintains that God is not focused on our past; we have created a god in our image who is past-present. We discover that this God of grace is future-present. As such, he appears to shift the whole conversation of our prayer to that focus.

As we engage with his discipleship of us, we experience adventure. Outrageous conversations invite us to outrageous dreams. And outrageous dreams become gloriously dangerous.

Prophecy

My wife and I joined the Eastgate School of Spiritual Life (ESSL) as students a few years ago. Immediately we found ourselves in a prophetic culture with prophets coaching us to prophesy to each other and to the people we met. This immersion in the prophecies I received not only gave me material to meditate upon before the Lord, but it also helped me reframe God's agenda, which was not so much about the past; it was more about my destiny.

As various prophecies came to pass, it reinforced my experience of God speaking to me specifically, and not only through the Bible. All of us in the school began to dream.

Dream Journal

> Go confidently in the direction of your dreams.
> Live the life you have imagined!
> **Henry David Thoreau**

> I sort of wonder at people with bucket lists. If there's been something I wanted to do, I just went and did it. I got nothing to put in some stupid bucket.
> **Dean Wesley Smith**
> Writing into the Dark

Andy and Janine Mason have done some brilliant work on what they call the Dream Culture.[27] Some have gone on to develop dream journals. Andy and Janine's advice, though, is more practical than only dreaming, and provides ways to deal with the roadblocks and tips about practical ways towards dream realisation.

Search on Amazon and a number of Dream Journals come up. I wonder, though, is soul journalling more comprehensive, more inclusive? It is bound to encapsulate whatever God wants us to pay attention to and wherever God wants to lead us. God, being future-present, will always lead us into dreaming and stepping into those dreams.

~~~~~~

PART 4 - MATERIALS

In this final part, we look at the pros and cons of handwriting versus digital soul journalling. And then some of the tools you can use to serve you as you soul journal.

> If you find yourself with the ball in the six-yard box and you're not sure what to do, just pop it in the net and we'll discuss your options afterwards.
> **Bill Shankly**
> former manager of Liverpool, talking to his strikers before a match

If you are reading this section because you are hesitating about jumping into soul journalling and you feel you need more information, you are probably wrong. My best advice is just get started, and review your materials later. Bill Shankly was right.

However, if you have been practising soul journalling for a few days and would like to go further, then read on.

CHAPTER 13

Handwriting Your Journal

You will have gathered by now that I'm an advocate of handwritten journalling. After spending a career in informations systems and related fields, I have learned to value the pen on the page. Here, I want to set out some of the relative strengths and weaknesses of handwriting (analog) versus typing (digital) your soul journal.

There seems to be a different emphasis of the same benefits between two different worlds of media: analog and digital. They may share the same benefits, but the weighting is different with each medium.

Here in this table is a comparison of the two worlds from my perspective, my weightings:

Benefits	Analog	Digital
Freedom from Distraction	+++	
Self-Awareness	+++	++
Clarity	+++	++
Focus	+++	++
State-Change	+++	+
Creativity of Expression	+++	+
Peace	+++	++
Joy	+++	++
Secure Storage	+++	++
Ease of Searching		+++

For me, the conclusion is clear: I lean to handwriting as a strong preference. For you, though, your weightings may well be different. Allow me, though to go further with this argument for pen and paper.

The Case for Analog Media

> Sometimes, I just want to get rid of all the technology and sit down in a quiet space with a pen and paper. There are so many apps out there and I feel like no one app gives me everything that I need. I've tried and really given them a go, doing those to-do lists of having your priorities or brain storming using lots of different apps … [but] when I get a pen and paper, or when I'm using my old-fashioned diary and pen, it just feels more flexible to me. I can always pull it out. I can focus.
>
> **Angela Cambrero, Australian entrepreneur**

Cambrero echoes my sentiment very well.

There are at least seven significant benefits I believe I can gain from handwriting. There are probably more. However, these are the key ones:

1.   Freedom in Handwriting

2.   Breaking the State

3.   Creative Self-Expression

4.   Peace on the Pen

5.   Joy

6.   Committed

7.   Separation from Work

1. Freedom in Handwriting

There is something very freeing about handwriting. It frees me from the context of complexity that I work within for so much of the time. Software gives me the structure it thinks I should follow. Have you ever found yourself becoming frustrated when you wanted to do something the app or program you happened to be using didn't seem to allow it?

Handwriting is truly freeform.

This freeform, in turn, resolves into something far more straightforward. It is not complicated. There are no passwords to remember, no apps to learn, no back-ups, version updates, or integration challenges with other apps to consider. The page will not go down on us. The worst that can happen is that we run out of ink or paper.

Once we have found our notebook, our pen or pencil, and a comfortable writing space, that's all we need. When we sit down to write, it's us, our pen and our paper, and the growing sense of his presence. We start to write.

Handwriting begins to detox us from constant distraction. This is freedom.

Here's an example from Nic Adams, showing how she uses a Harry Potter notebook, and focuses here on declarations:

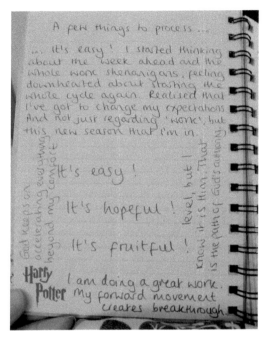

Notice, Nic begins: "A few things to process…" Her journal becomes somewhere to meditate and mull over her internal narratives in a very positive way.

2. Breaking the State

Handwriting is much more visceral. Moving from screen to pen becomes a physical clue that breaks the state of being too screen-focused, perhaps, in a detailed task. Our state changes as we move to a physical notebook, where it can be more standing back from our habitual routines.

This stepping out of the stream of computer-based work into something, perhaps more deliberate, can be very positive in our working patterns. Because of the visceral nature of handwriting, there is a much more immediate connection between us and the words we write.

Very few still use a typewriter, so we nearly always type on a computer keyboard. Writing on a computer feels, for me, somewhat more detached from what I handwrite. Here's that pivotal moment, again, in the parable of the Lost Son:

> And he was longing to be fed with pods that the
> pigs ate, and no one gave him anything.
>
> But when he came to himself, he said, 'How many of
> my father's hired servants have more than enough
> bread, but I perish here with hunger!'
> **Luke 15: 16-17**

From self-awareness and clarity comes an ability to move out of our emotional narrative and experience an entirely different perspective. Like the prodigal son, who came to himself, we too, can experience with the shift out of our habitual way of working and thinking, we can step into quite a different perspective.

The act of journalling can allow us to break the state, as Neurolinguistic Programming (NLP) calls it: changing what we do and focus upon, it suddenly allows a very different conversation within ourselves. This shift to another state becomes a delight.

The state we are in is more than the rational case we make for understanding the world around us; it involves our emotions. We make sense of the world around us in frames of thinking, not as a set of individual facts. Our confirmation bias[28] is always hard at work in hunting for evidence that corroborates our current frame of understanding. However, most of the time, our frame of understanding, our paradigm, is faulty. We need to reconnect with the Truth (John 14:6).

> But when I thought how to understand this,
> it seemed to me a wearisome task,
> until I went into the sanctuary of God;
> then I discerned their end.
> **Psalm 73:16-17**

This verse is another pivotal point in a brutally honest song of David, where he is confused about the evil in the world and why evil-doers appear to flourish. He encountered that state-change upon entering the sanctuary of God, a physical change to where he was.

As I work in front of a screen in much of my work, moving to my notebook with a pen helps me break the state so that I can more ably enter that sanctuary.

There is a traditional stream of spirituality that uses the concept of the *sacrament*. A sacrament is an outward sign of inward grace; something you do physically that mirrors a powerful unseen spiritual reality. Baptism, breaking bread, confession and the marriage ceremony are all recognised as sacraments, in many Christian traditions. So, we do something physically because it symbolises something profound that we are doing in the spiritual.

For me, in this sense, there is a sacrament from moving from the screen to my paper journal and my ink pen. It is sacramental for me because I am going into the sanctuary of God to have a conversation with him.

3. Creative Self-Expression

With handwriting, it is easier to switch off our Inner Critic, long enough for creativity to flow.

Many times, we will discover that the very act of physically writing our thoughts down, maybe doodling, begins to unravel a problem. We are away from the screen. It is harder to be distracted in front of a physical page. Of course, we can work hard to remove all electronic distractions but, with a pen and notebook, that is just not an issue.

Then there is something else…

4. Peace on the Pen

Closely associated with freedom and state-change, is a sublime sense of peace. This particular channel of peace is partly a by-product of the pace of handwriting; it slows us down. Handwriting is less frenetic. I know that practices of mindfulness help many people. However, it seems to me that prayerful writing gains most, if not all of the benefits of mindfulness... and then some.

Most people when they search for peace, seek the absence of noise. When we are in joyful focus, we find an activity like handwriting displaces so much, that a sense of peace is a beautiful side effect.

The pace of the online world is fast. Handwriting is not, and this aids purposeful meditation. It helps us adjust to a different tempo.

Consider this meditation, which came out of my prayer journal:

> Of the increase of his government and of peace
> there will be no end,
> on the throne of David and over his kingdom,
> to establish it and to uphold it
> with justice and with righteousness
> from this time forth and forever more.
> The zeal of the LORD of hosts will do this.
> **Isaiah 9:7 (ESV)**

I used to think of peace as something binary; that is, you either have it or you don't. This verse prophesies a kingdom and peace increasing without end. There is an inner peace that can grow and deepen. This dimension of peace moves us from operating from survival, from an orphan mindset to one where we know the riches that are ours in communion with our heavenly Father. This inner peace does not motivate us to act from survival any more but from a strong sense of growing hope.

In the same way, as his kingdom extends regionally, external threats reduce and humankind discovers the possibility to recreate, to find purpose and significance in working for and with God.

Then, there is that close neighbour of Peace, which is Joy:

5. Joy

Julia Cameron, that great teacher of creative writing, wrote a book entitled *The Sound of Paper*. What some of us have come to connect with is the sheer joy of writing: the pleasure of using our preferred stationery.

Unlike some sterile keyboard, handwriting can be a means for us to connect with an immediate physical pleasure as well as a deeper delight of the journey it can take in our heart and mind. The voice of the Pharisee within us is now weak enough for us to laugh at, and ignore, the voice that says, *But this shouldn't be pleasurable!*

Part of the joy is in expressing **creativity**. Before our eyes, we see the fruits of our imagination forming words, sentences, diagrams and arguments; there is nothing like it. There is the joy in writing that is shared by all artists. It becomes a pleasure of the medium of creativity. Maybe that joy is the rediscovery that we were born to create. Maybe it's the other way around: rediscovering our creativity is our route to joy. Maybe it is just a virtuous circle, where joy and creativity reinforce each other.

Also, there is something deliciously private about handwriting; it is between us and the paper. This is a private joy.

However, let's not rush on to the other benefits too quickly. Let's stay with joy for a moment longer.

Remember, the joy of writing has a powerful intrinsic motivation. We allow ourselves to connect with this, and the writing habit becomes unstoppable. We shift from feeling we *have* to journal to *wanting* to journal. We make sure our environment is adequately arranged for experiencing that pleasure. Moreover, we remember that our God is the source of all true pleasure. Here's an extract from *The Screwtape Letters*, letters from a senior devil (Screwtape) to a junior devil talking about God:

> "He's a hedonist at heart. All those fasts and vigils and stakes and crosses are only a facade. Or only like foam on the sea shore. Out at sea, out in His sea, there is pleasure, and more pleasure. He makes no secret of it; at His right hand are 'pleasures for evermore.'"
>
> **C.S.Lewis**
> The Screwtape Letters

Handwriting becomes unashamedly hedonistic. We handwrite, and we grow to love it. We find it's a good antidote to the religious spirit, particularly to performance religion.

How does joy arise in us? For me, it is a combination of causes that conspire to lift my heart, of several of the other benefits on this list: the tactile nature of handwriting, for one; the emergent flow of self-expression, is another; as is the freedom that handwriting gives me.

So we find in our experience of handwritten soul journalling the following: Freedom, State-Change, Creative Self-Expression, Peace and Joy.

However, there is another particularly profound benefit of handwriting, some would say the most important one. At first, that benefit can seem like a negative constraint. But this particular constraint is glorious.

6. Committed

The constraint is that, unlike digital media, when I handwrite in ink, **I cannot edit what I have written**; at least, I cannot edit easily. It's a faff. So, I don't try.

More to the point, when we learn **not** to edit on-the-go as we express ourselves on the page, it releases a kind of freedom we just do not experience with digital writing. If we are writing on a word processor app, the temptation to edit is hard to resist.

As I explored in the chapter on **The Perfect Lie**, creative self-expression requires us all to allow the Inner Creative within us to flow forth. Our Inner Critic needs to leave. It is not required.

Many see the ability to edit as they write as a big advantage; and it is, in so many ways; that is true. However, I do not see this as a benefit for soul journalling. Remember, when we soul journal, we write for ourselves and for God alone. We are talking with ourselves and the Lord. But if we think that God is going to be our copy editor, then we need to think again.

So, *not* being able to edit becomes a huge advantage to us, in that we begin to suspend the need to edit ourselves. With practice, we will find the media frees us to flow. Therein lies much of the power of handwritten soul journalling.

7. Separation from Work

I write for a living. I author blog articles, videos, books (like this one), courses and workshops. I compose my work, including this book, using digital software on the screen. If I'm not physically meeting someone face-to-face, or facilitating or teaching before a group people who are present in the room, then I am usually working on and through my computer.

So, another reason I prefer to keep my soul journal by handwriting is that I am a writer. Since I use my computers for work, shifting to analog helps me stay focused on the audience of me and God. Whereas, composing on the screen is, for me, work.

> And they heard the sound of the LORD God walking in the garden in the cool of the day, and the man and his wife hid themselves from the presence of the LORD God among the trees of the garden. But the LORD God called to the man and said to him, "Where are you?"
> **Genesis 3:8-9**

I'm guessing this wasn't the first time God went out to walk with the first man and woman in the cool of the day. No doubt, the man and woman talked with their Creator on previous occasions about the last day's work and the work they might do in the day ahead, but, at those times, they were not working; they were walking in the presence. Then shame came upon them, and they fled from his presence.

When most of us handwrite, it is not part of our usual working practice. But our handwriting can, and often does, lead to better work.

So, for me, shifting to pen and paper keeps that separation. As Joni Mitchell sang so prophetically — whether she knew it or not — in her song, Woodstock:

We've got to get back to the garden.

Summary: Benefits of the Handwritten Journal

Handwritten journalling is particularly helpful in:

✓   Freeing ourselves from external distractions and complexities

✓   Moving away from screen time to pen and paper can trigger a vital
     state-change in our thinking; it can help us shift in our awareness
     so that it becomes more like entering the sanctuary

✓   Developing creative self-expression, because handwriting does
     not allow us to edit on-the-go, so that we focus instead on the
     expressive process, rather than on trying to produce good copy

✓   Reconnecting with a sense of peace. Handwriting is slower, less
     frenetic, so it allows us to connect with peace more easily

✓   Experiencing joy, through a more intimately physical connection
     with what we write than through a keyboard

✓   What we handwrite is committed to paper immediately. So we
     give up trying to edit ourselves

✓   As a digital author, handwriting helps me separate my written
     conversations from work; and it is likely to be the same for you too

So, what about digital soul journalling? In the next chapter, I share some
thoughts about how you can make that work for you as well.

CHAPTER 14
The Digital Soul Journal

You could make the case that all of the benefits I have attributed to handwriting in that earlier chapter, could be gained by writing on a computer. True, but they might be harder to attain.

So, here I want to offer you some ways of doing this through digital tools. Also, I give you some warnings if you still prefer to go with digital media.

Digital Tools

There are multiple writing apps, of course, and these are changing all the time. So, do bear in mind that much of this list will be out of date almost as soon as this book is published. It is the nature of the digital world to move fast, so this is very much a *point in time assessment*.

The two main factors to bear in mind about your choice of writing tool are in order:

✓ Use the tools you are **already using** and that you are **already used to using**. You don't want the distraction during reflective writing of having to learn how to use a new tool. The key is to create, as far as possible, a frictionless writing experience. For most people, this will lean them towards a common tool like Microsoft Word.

✓ Prefer a tool that has a **full screen writing mode**, with nothing else visible but what you write. Many tools do offer this, and it is well worth finding out how to operate this way.

My Current List

Microsoft Word (Most Platforms)

I recommend Word because of the interface. Like it or not, Word has established itself as the user interface which other word processors imitate or are measured against. I have noticed that when we try to make sense of any new text-based program, most of us look for similarities with Word.

Alternatives:

- **Apple Pages** (Mac & IOS): a very good, stable product.

- **Google Docs** (Web & client versions on most devices) This is a strong platform, but encourages online use, which can be more vulnerable to distractions.

Scrivener (Mac, Windows, IOS)

Unlike Word, Scrivener has multiple other features and views, but can be used in full screen. If you haven't used Scrivener before, don't use it for journalling; it has a steep learning curve.

However, once you master Scrivener, it can be a great vehicle for journalling. For me, Scrivener is the Ferrari of word processors; it allows me, among many other things, to go Full Screen Composition Mode, so that all I can see on the screen is my writing.

Evernote (Mac, Windows, IOS, Android)

If you are used to Evernote, then it can make a good platform for writing and storing your journal. I would recommend creating a separate notebook for your journal entries, which can be password protected. I have used Evernote this way in the past. Also, note that my practice of Bi-Modal Soul Journalling ultimately captures my handwritten entries by being scanned into Evernote.

Alternatives:

- **Microsoft OneNote** (most platforms): in terms of functions, it is a close competitor to Evernote. In some respects it has some better features than Evernote, but it is limited to use with a Microsoft Office account.

Other Journalling Apps

These show you the range of apps on offer. However, I would be cautious about recommending some to these, for all the reasons I've already discussed around the sources of distraction; some of these apps come with other so-called 'features' that, for me, get in the way of focused self-expression.

- Day One (Mac, iOS, Android)—best for writing quick journal entries in a simple, intuitive interface

- Diarium (Windows, Android)—best for dictating journal entries and seamless integration with Windows

- Glimpses (Windows)—best for free journalling on Windows; free

- Journey (Mac, Windows, iOS, Android, Chrome OS, Web)—best for seamless journalling and syncing on any platform

- Penzu (Web, iOS, Android)—best for journalling in a blog-like environment while keeping your entries secure

- Dabble.me (Email)—more suitable for journalling by email

- Momento (iOS)—best for automated journalling from your social media feeds

- Grid Diary (iOS)—best for templated journalling

- Five Minute Journal (iOS, Android)—best for quick morning and evening reflections

Onwards

I suspect… there is no end game.

> So he started out, and on his way he met an Ethiopian
> eunuch… When they came up out of the water, the Spirit
> of the Lord suddenly took Philip away, and the eunuch
> did not see him again, but went on his way rejoicing.
> **Acts 8: 27a, 39**

M y story is an emergent one. So is yours. We are discovering this amazing journey, and it is particularly exciting because we do not know what the end game is. I suspect, with an infinite God, there is no end game.

So, if I were to write this book again in a few years, it would be different. That is the glorious dynamic for all of us in following Jesus. There's so much more to learn and to explore about this amazing God, his Kingdom and his plans for us.

If you are further on with your soul journalling than I am, then please write to me at **soul2page.com**. Wherever you are in exploring prayer and conversations with God through your journal, please write to me anyway. Let's encourage one another. You will also find some additional tips and recources.

Thank you for journeying with me for this part of the way.

Every blessing to you as you grow in the knowledge and love of our Saviour.

Endnotes

Preface

Chapter 1- Hello?

1   *Too Busy Not to Pray: Slowing Down to Be with God.*

2   *The Power of Habit: Why We Do What We Do and How to Change It.*

3   *Opening Up by Writing It Down: How Expressive Writing*

I   *mproves Health and Eases Emotional Pain.*

Chapter 2 - Noise

4   For example, see the chapter called *Code Wars*, in Tom de Marco and Tim Lister's book, *Peopleware: Productive Projects and Teams.*

5   Cal Newport, *Deep Work*

6   Charles Hummel, *Tyranny of the Urgent*

7   I write about this and how to deal with it more extensively in my previous book, *Leading Yourself: Succeeding from*

t   *he Inside Out.*

8   *"Yes" or "No": The Guide to Better Decisions: A Story.*

Chapter 3 - Hearing

9   *Man's Search for Meaning: The Classic Tribute to Hope from the Holocaust.*

10   *The Neuroscience of Leadership,* by David Rock & Jeffrey Schwartz, Strategy & Business, Summer 2006, Issue 43.

Chapter 4 - Starting

11   James Clear, *Atomic Habits: An Easy and Proven Way to Build Good Habits and Break Bad Ones,*

12   There is some evidence that suggests that the ambient noise of a coffee shop is helpful to focus and do thought-intensive work. I can vouch for that in my own experience.

Chapter 5 - Growing

13   *Peopleware, op cit.*

14   One of the popular texting applications I use is WhatsApp. This par
        ticular app comes with a desktop tool that can synchronise with the
        phone's account and messages. It allows me to compose messages on
        my desktop computer, which is a much better composition experience
        for me.

15   This was part of a UK GCSE Revision Notes series published by
        Hodder & Stoughton. I was commissioned to create the Mind Maps
        for Physics, Chemistry, Biology and Double Science.

16   Mark Appleyard, *Think, Speak, Live: Business from Heaven's Perspec
        tive.*

Chapter 6 - The Perfect Lie

17   Stephen Pressfield, *The War of Art.*

18   Julia Cameron, *The Artist's Way: A Course in Discovering
and Recovering Your Creative Self.*

Chapter 7 - Abundance

19   In Part 3-Making Sense of All This.

20   Daniel Kahneman, *Thinking, Fast and Slow.*

Chapter 8 - Media

21   Clive Thompson, https://youtu.be/89vzfTFu1Vw

22   Ryder Carroll has his own website for the bullet journal:

        http://bulletjournal.com/

Chapter 9 - Blessings

23   *The Power of Habit,* op.cit.

24   michaelhyatt.com

25   *Time to Think: Listening to Ignite the Human Mind.*

Chapter 10 - Soul

26   See Wendy Backlund's *Living from the Unseen.*

Chapter 12 - Future

27   *Dream Culture: Bringing Dreams to Life..*

28   Another of the biases identified by Kahneman, op.cit.

Appendix

Further Resources

Websites

Soul2Page.com

I have created a website with some resources that I hope will help you in a way that a book or ebook cannot. It will link you with a community of like-minded people and with some online resources that will help you go deeper.

PatrickMayfield.com

This is my main site, which includes a free email course on writing and publishing.

Some Key References

Throughout this book I have referenced some key sources that have shaped my own approach.

Prayer Journalling

Bill Hybels, *Too Busy Not to Pray: Slowing Down to Be with God* (1998, InterVarsity Press).

Self-Leadership

Stephen R. Covey, *Principle-Centered Leadership* (1992, Free Press).

Patrick Mayfield, *Leading Yourself: Succeeding from the Inside Out* (2016, Elbereth)

Emotional Healing through Writing

James W. Pennebaker & Joshua M. Smythe, *Opening Up by Writing It Down: How Expressive Writing Improves Health and Eases Emotional Pain* (2016, Guildford Press)

The Soul and It's Transformation

Steve Backlund, *You're Crazy if You Don't Talk to Yourself* (2012) and

Declarations: Unlocking Your Future (2013, Igniting Hope Ministries)

Wendy Backlund, *Living from the Unseen: Reflections from a Transformed Life* (2012, Igniting Hope Ministries); and

Victorious Emotions: Creating a Framework for a Happier You (2017, Igniting Hope Ministries)

Joyce Meyer, *Battlefield of the Mind: Winning the Battle of Your Mind: Winning the Battle in Your Mind* (1995, Hodder)

Curt Thompson MD, *The Anatomy of the Soul: Surprising connections between neuro science and spiritual practices that can transform your life and relationships* (2010, Tyndale Momentum)

Mark and Patti Virkler, *Dialogue with God: Opening the door to two-way prayer* (1986, Bridge-Logos)

Andrew Wommack, *Spirit, Soul and Body* (2010, Harrison House)

SOAP Journalling

Mark Appleyard, *Think, Speak Live: Business from Heaven's Perspective* (2017, Anothen)

Wayne Cordeiro, *The Divine Mentor: Growing Your Faith as You Sit at the Feet of the Savior* (2007, Bethany House Publishers)

Deep Thinking

Daniel Kahneman, *Thinking, Fast and Slow* (2011, Farrar, Straus and Giroux)

Cal Newport, *Deep Work: Rules for Focused Success in a Distracted World* (2016, Grand Central Publishing)

Habits & How to Form or Break Them

James Clear, *Atomic Habits: An Easy and Proven Way to Build Good Habits and Break Bad Ones*, (2018, Avery)

Charles Duhigg, *The Power of Habit: Why We Do What We Do, and How To Change It* (2013, Random House)

Writing

Julia Cameron, *The Artist's Way: A Course in Discovering and Recovering Your Creative Self*, (1992, Tarcher)

Frankl, Viktor, *Man's Search for Meaning: The Classic Tribute to Hope from the Holocaust.* (1959, Random House)

Also: *The Sound of Paper: Starting from Scratch*, (2004, Tarcher)

Annie Lamott, *Bird by Bird: Some Instructions on Writing and Life*, (1995, Anchor)

Steven Pressfield and Shawn Coyne, *The War of Art: Break Through the Blocks and Win Your Inner Creative Battles* (2012, Black Irish Entertainment LLC)

Dreaming

Bill Johnson, *Dreaming with God: Secrets to Redesigning Your World Through God's Creative Flow* (2006, Destiny Image)

Matthew Kelly, *The Dream Manager*, (2007, Beacon Publishing)

Andy and Janine Mason, *Dream Culture: Bringing Dreams to Life*, (2011, River) t

With Special Thanks to:

There are so many people who helped me that there is a real risk that I forget to mention and thank them. These friends have contributed to this book so that it is much, much better than it might have been.

I'd like to thank Eastgate, an extraordinary community of faith, hope and love, that continually calls me to live up to my true identity and introduces me to new realms of freedom and courage. In particular, I'd like to acknowledge and thank David Webster, and Vicky Schulz, both of whom have commented on drafts and have generally built into me through ESSL and now as friends. For example, Vicky made the suggestion that the book could do with activations, and she contributed many of these. Also, Mark Hendley has become a dear friend who inspired my wife and I last year in leading our party to Israel.

Sasha Caridia and Nicole Adams both contributed their journals as well as feeding back comments on early drafts.

Richard Smith has become a valued friend, who gave me much food for thought whilst being incredibly encouraging.

Jamie and Rachel Lee are an honour to know and to collaborate with. At the time of writing, they were also generous enough to ask me to review a work they were undertaking.

Rob Schulz has been a faithful friend, challenging some things, but encouraging me greatly. Katy Dusting, who went through the Eastgate School of Spiritual Life with my wife and I has been a constant source of wise support, helping me with the spiritual direction perspective on this.

Finally, thanks to my wife, Felicity, for reading and re-reading seemingly endless drafts and encouraging me to finish this project. I am rich in loving, wise friends, who believe in me.

Of course, blame me, and only me, for any shortcomings or errors in this book. I am, after all, a lifelong learner.

Patrick

About the Author

Patrick Mayfield has spent his career in town planning, IT, project support, as a freelance consultant, running a training & consultancy business, facilitator, coach, author of two previous books, and a contributing author of several more. He began as a head altar boy in a convent. Over time he was a Baptist deacon, a house church leader, was Chair of Willow Creek Association UK, and, until he moved to Kent, a lay preacher in an Anglican church, .

He and his wife, Felicity, moved to Kent to be part of Eastgate, and now Heaven in Healthcare. They have six grown-up children and eight grandchildren.

In the words of the late John Wimber, Patrick hopes to grow up before he grows old. His children tell him it's too late!

Other Books by Patrick Mayfield

Practical People Engagement: Leading Change by the Power of Relationships

Leading Yourself: Succeeding from the Inside Out

Lightning Source UK Ltd.
Milton Keynes UK
UKHW020052130422
401470UK00006B/1439